The Empowered Child

The Empowered Child

Raising Conscious, Confident & Connected Kids

MARY TAN

NEW YORK

LONDON • NASHVILLE • MELBOURNE • VANCOUVER

Advance Praise

"*The Empowered Child* is an amazing book! It is is jam-packed with valuable insight on conscious parenting. Throughout this book, Mary constantly keeps you in the question, forcing you to reflect deeply, keeping you mindful and aware, ultimately connecting you back to your heart and deep within the soul; where all your best parenting lies. It's a refreshing journey down a beautiful road of mindful parenting."

~Alex Urbina
Teen & Parenting Expert, Transformational Life Coach &
Author of *The Inspirational Parent*

"Mary Tan has raised the bar and given parents an incredibly honest vision of the amazing privilege and opportunity that parenting offers each of us. If you want your child to uniquely stand out as themselves, offering their best to the world, then the game plan is here. I celebrate her gifted perspective and service."

~Dr. Ron Stotts
Author of *Overscheduled By Success: A Guide for Transformational Leaders*

"During these transitional and ever-changing times, parents and teachers are constantly searching for tools for their children and students to expand their consciousness and leave their indelible mark on this planet. Mary Tan offers guidance for those who wish to understand the purpose of their children's gifts, and teach them to stand in their power, live honestly and truthfully, and enjoy life in the process."

~Harriette Knight
Master Healer, Author, and Radio Host

"I first met Mary at an event I attended in 2008. As I entered the room, her "Goddess Energy" was evident! I reached out and shared what I experienced, and she had this smile that is piercing to the soul and said, "Thank You!" I have been blessed to have shared the stage with Mary along this journey and have the upmost deserved respect for her. As I was reading *The Empowered Child*, I was amazed of how Mary shed light on how society has programmed us and how it effects our youth today. Because of Mary's book, I found the inspiration to be more involved with the change for our youth and focus on their talents and to be more, do more, and share more. I believe *The Empowered Child* will do the same for you! As you read more of this amazing book you have in your hands, you realize Mary is the "Real Deal" and is walking her talk!

You will benefit from her insights, wisdom, and inspiration that she has gathered over the years, which she now shares with you in this book. Buckle up and enjoy!"

~Ruben Mata
International Speaker, Trainer, Author, Founder of
StandDevelopmentFoundation.com

"Mary Tan is a powerful teacher of empowerment and a wonderful, caring mom. Her book, The Empowered Child, is chock full of thoughtful, rich, practical information for all parents who would like to raise an empowered child, especially those who are parenting passionate, spirited children. I highly recommend it!"

~Wendy Silvers
The Awakened Mother Coach, Founder of
Million Mamas Movement

The Empowered Child
Raising Conscious, Confident and Connected Kids

Published in New York, New York, by Morgan James Publishing in partnership with Difference Press. Morgan James is a trademark of Morgan James, LLC. www.MorganJamesPublishing.com

The Morgan James Speakers Group can bring authors to your live event. For more information or to book an event visit The Morgan James Speakers Group at www.TheMorganJamesSpeakersGroup.com.

ISBN 9781642791327 paperback
ISBN 9781642791334 eBook
Library of Congress Control Number: 2018947952

Cover & Interior Design by:
Christopher Kirk
GFSstudio.com

In an effort to support local communities, raise awareness and funds, Morgan James Publishing donates a percentage of all book sales for the life of each book to Habitat for Humanity Peninsula and Greater Williamsburg.

Get involved today! Visit
www.MorganJamesBuilds.com

For my husband, Adrian, who supported me as only a twin flame and twin oak could. This is especially for my daughters, Arianna and Angelina, for inspiring me to be my very best for them and the future generations of the planet.

Table of Contents

Introduction

"Under any circumstance, simply do your best and you will avoid self-judgment, self-abuse and regret."
–Don Miguel Ruiz

I was inspired to write this book because in all my years as an empowerment coach, I have seen how challenging it is to undo the traumas of the past. Now that I have two little girls of my own, I was compelled to repurpose all the tools I've gathered to offer them a shortened learning curve to living an authentic life of happiness and success. Before becoming a wife and mom, I made a personal choice to transform my past pains into the greatest gifts of empowerment. Now as a mom looking into the future, it is my duty to offer the gems of my path. This is why I write. It is my hope to share what has worked in my career and personal life so you may benefit. Everyone encounters heartbreak and challenges. If I can find the diamonds in the rough and share the glimmer of hope from its shine, then it was all worthwhile.

CHAPTER 1

At Wit's End

"A lot of what is most beautiful about
the world arises from struggle."
–Malcolm Gladwell

Remember when you were pregnant and glowing with the joys of life flowing through your body? Your skin was amazing; your hair was thick and shiny. All of your highest hopes and dreams were formulating right there in your belly. What no one ever talked about was how truly difficult it is to raise a child. It's not all giggles and hugs. There are some seriously challenging times that require the right mindset, perspective, and tools to bring everyone to higher ground. In fact, having a tribe of women around you as you journey through this phase is priceless.

Is your child your greatest love, yet she sometimes drives you absolutely mad with intense and unexpected emotional breakdowns? She's the center of your world, and there's no doubt you are grateful to have her in your life. But there are those moments where something seems really off with how she freaks out over the smallest things. Then, there are additional times when she's so difficult and strong willed, you want to pull your hair out. The hair that's turning grey from stress? Other kids don't seem to have those same intense reactions. What's up with that?

Or maybe your husband is at the end of his rope losing his patience easily after all these years of oscillating hypersensitivity and strong-willed behavior. It's stressful, draining, and exhausting. Right about now everyone is feeling the negative energy dragging them down into the dumps. It's even putting a strain on your marriage. You know your child is sweet and loving. Yet, when seemingly insignificant triggers send her into a screaming episode, you're left wondering what the hell went wrong? Emotions pivot so quickly, it's hard to keep up. Are you doing a good job as a mom? Do you even know what you're doing? These are questions you might be asking yourself and, I assure you, if you're reading this book, you are definitely on the right track. There are no accidents. You were ready to hear something that is here for you. I'm so glad you decided to pick up this book to empower yourself, your child, and your family.

You're doing a great job. You know why I can say that without ever chatting with you? The fact that you're choosing to use your time to improve yourself through a book tells me so. On top of that, I know that everyone does the best they can with the tools they have at the time. There is no right or wrong in life. Only feedback. So, put your self-judgment to the side for now and pick it up later if you wish. For now, put it all into a box, lock it up, and place it outside the space where you are sitting while reading this book.

Now that we've established the fact that you're a good mom, a great mom even, and becoming the mom you want to be all the time, let's get back to it. Your kid is hyper- sensitive. Without warning, normal everyday situations can send her spiraling out of control and it's leaving you at wit's end. Other times, she's extremely strong willed, won't listen and it takes all of your energy to try and stay calm. You've tried all kinds of methods and tactics and have even used practices that weren't necessarily aligned with your values, but you were willing to give everything at least one try. I understand. It's not easy being a mom. In fact, it's the most demanding job that requires an incredible amount of energy, intention, and awareness. There are a million books out there, but you haven't found the manual on how to help your strong willed yet, hypersensitive child through her challenges so everyone feels empowered in the end. And in today's information age, sifting through all the data alone is overwhelming.

It's strange. You look at other children and you don't think they are going through the same challenges that you are. I mean, you've talked to tons of moms and asked them straight out. Maybe you find one or two who can relate, but on the inside, you feel alone, like an island. It feels lonely as if no one else is going through what you're experiencing, like you can't talk about it because either you'll sound like you're complaining, ungrateful, or a bad mom. You feel isolated because you can't relate to other moms and you wish you could have a tribe of women who get you. Well, guess what sister? You found us. If, at the end of the book, you feel like you have been seen, heard, and understood, then for sure you've found your soul sister tribe. We've been waiting for you. Don't fret ever again, you hear me? Mothering is challenging. Of course, it is! You're guiding a whole new being into the world and praying to God that you do a good enough job not to mess this child up. You can try, but I bet she'll still blame you somewhere along the line. It's all good though. You can't eliminate her inevitable lessons in life. You can only offer her the information, guidance, and presence. The rest is up to her.

Kahlil Gibran, one of my favorite poets, writes that children may come through us, but they don't belong to us. His wise words say, "Your children are not your children. They are the sons and daughters of Life's longing for itself. They come through you but not from you, and though they are with you yet they belong not to you." It's a gorgeous poem that is timeless and holds the vibration of eternal truths. To me, this means you are to do your best to guide them with love and consciousness knowing that, ultimately, they are their own person.

What do you do when a girlfriend calls you crying on the phone? You immediately drop everything and are listening with all ears, right? Your heart goes out to her. "What's wrong honey?" you ask with such compassion and interest. Why is she upset and what caused it? You want to know so you can offer words of encouragement or simply hold the space for her to feel safe enough to let it all out. Being seen and heard is so powerful. That alone can heal the situation and allow her to exhale, feel the emotions, leave her space, and pick herself back up to move forward. Other times, being seen was helpful, but more processing needs to happen internally to transcend whatever learning was available for her in that moment. What if we took this energy and approach into dealing with our sensitive children? Rather than play the same old record of feeling frustrated, angry, disappointed, helpless, hopeless, and powerless, do something totally different. Maybe you've done this before, but it's been awhile and this serves a timely reminder. Get down to her level and hold the loving space like you would for your girlfriend on the phone. Everything is energy and vibration. If you do that, I guarantee your child will feel you. When she picks up the unconditional love in your gaze, she will melt and shift from the impact of feeling accepted and loved even when she's acting at her very *worst*. When she doesn't shift and you continue to hold the space for her to do what she needs to do without the pressure of a time limit, eventually she will see you and gratitude will fill her heart. Do this over and over again and soon your world will change.

CHAPTER 2

Kicking and Screaming

"The whole world opens when we
accept this moment, this very moment."
–Deepak Chopra

Just in case you think I don't understand the situation, check out this scene. After spending the day working, I walked into my house greeted by five-year-old Arianna face down on the living room floor screaming, crying, kicking, and flailing. This could have been a shocking moment, but I have become accustomed to this behavior. I didn't say it was easy, although it does get easier the more I stay the course. Her needs are different and the tactics to support her through it are naturally different, as well. Using fear and making threats of taking things away as a way to control a child's behavior might initially get the result you want, but in the long run, it will not work in your favor. Here's why.

Many times, when adults have a plan in their minds of what it is they want to accomplish in that moment, they use the adult way to communicate to children. You have to remember that these are kids who are learning an immense amount of socio-emotional skills at this stage. Not only that, they are learning and absorbing all this data at school and bombarded with information from the world around them at all times. They are learning how to use their body, what hurts it, what it feels like to have a cold, to heal, and to exist in a body. They are learning about feelings. What are feelings? What's the anatomy of it, why does it feel that way and why is it so damn scary sometimes? What are they supposed to do about it to feel better? She starts to wonder, "Why does everyone get mad when I'm having a hard day?" She'll make up the belief that it's not OK to be herself, that it's not OK to feel and process these enormous emotions, that the only way to be loved is to push it down and plaster a happy smile on top of the wound. Isn't that why the world today is breaking down in every arena? Isn't it true that what we learn at childhood becomes the script for adulthood? So, how's that working for us today on a global scale? Are we as a human race happy or tortured? And if you're tired of the state of world affairs, isn't it time we do something different from the start?

Just because something has been taught once or several times doesn't mean the child necessarily gets it on a deeper level. Even adults are still learning how to deal with emotions, interpersonal interactions, and how to be effective in this world. So, the level of pressure and expectation that parents place on children is astronomical and back-breaking. If the kid is happy-go-lucky, then the adult is happy and might even pat herself on the back thinking, "I've done a great job parenting." If the kid is face down on the ground having a high-level tantrum at five years old, then the parent may be able to muster up a small amount of patience allotted for these draining episodes. Many things are at play here, though.

So, as I walked into the house greeted by little Arianna screaming on the ground, the two-year-old Gigi was unsure how to be in the energy and the sitter was standing in the corner wondering, "What the heck is going on here?" I come in knowing this scene is begging for a loving leader to facilitate a transformation for the family. I find a place to put my things down and immediately sit near her. Close, but not too close. This is done to honor her energetic bubble. It lets her know my support is accessible upon request and her raging behavior is accepted. It lets her know I am respecting her space and process without placing any expectations on her. This offers her the chance to go through the tantrum without interruption. When she starts to flip the corner of the rug over with her feet, something I usually ask her not to do, I knew right away she was looking for buttons to trigger in me to bring on a conflict. From the outside someone could easily misjudge the situation. The mom appears to be too lenient and the child unruly. The child could be mistaken for being weak, bratty or manipulating. Here, Arianna was looking for an adult to offer the resistance to her tantrum so she could have an excuse to really let her emotions rage. She was picking a fight so she had an outlet for her big emotions. But I didn't give in because I recognized what was happening. When she realized I wasn't going to push back, she went to the next person she could rile up. She wanted to push the boundaries to see if anything she did would cause others not to love her. I breathed in unconditional love, exhaled it energetically into her space and repeated this for the entire session. It took 20 minutes to reach a transformation. It felt like a much longer period and, in the past, it certainly took a lot longer until I started to get better at coaching her through these intense emotions. Luckily, I have a lot of tools I've been using for more than ten years coaching adults. As soon as I realized my role as a coach in her life, these moments really shifted. You are your child's coach, too. I'll teach you the best tools via the EMPOWER Method so everyone feels elevated in the end. It's what we teach at the Light Warrior School and to parents journeying through this phase of a child's learning curve. That's all it is. The child is learning how to be in this world and you get the opportunity to show her what it all means and how to use it to her benefit. Before we dive deep into each one, here is a summary of the steps:

E: Evaluate the Situation. Did something happen in that moment? Has she not eaten in the last two hours and is having low blood sugar? Did she have good quality sleep last night? Is there an age appropriate challenge she's learning through? Is she injured? Maybe the breakdown is due to months of pent-up unprocessed emotions.

M: Make Yourself Available. Just like you would pause to listen to a crying friend on the phone, pause and make yourself available through your body, listening, and energy. Come down to her eye level. Listen with an open heart full of non-judgmental curiosity. Be fully present with your energy. Turn off the stove, mute the phone, turn off the music. Be here now.

P: Put On Your Coaching Hat. You wear many hats. During an emotional breakdown, remember to put on your coaching hat. There is no judgment, shaming or blaming. You are the person on higher ground who holds the vision for the child who's emotionally hurting to break through to the other side.

O: Offer a Safe Space. Physically make the space around her safer if she's having a physical tantrum and thrashing about. If she wants to punch and scream then either make that space supportive of that or bring her somewhere that has the soft components of pillows and blankets to do so fully. Energetically, put on the dome, ground it, and connect it to Source energy. Repeat that for each body. Breathe unconditional love in and out through your soul space. Blanket the scene with love and compassion.

W: Wait For the First Move. After making your non-invasive, non-threatening presence available and known, wait for her lead. Bear witness to her process and watch to make sure her body stays safe. Bring the silent energy of readiness and support as you observe the emotional arc from beginning to end. Avoid counting the minutes because that will make it last forever. Drop into the present moment and breathe.

E: Elevate the Vibrational Energy. As you're serving her by holding the space as a witness, you can elevate the vibration of the scenario energetically. Call in the angels and unseen helpers. Pray for Source to show everyone the way. Fill the space with even more universal love. Use your mind's eye to pull out the negative energies from her or the space and throw it into a blue alchemical fire in the corner of the room. Negative energies aren't evil or scary. It is simply a vibratory level that registers lower on the scale of emotions. Keep it up as you hold space for her transformation.

R: Review What Just Happened. Once the session has completed, naturally she will likely want to come in for a hug. Whether she does or not is all good. She just had an intense emotional breakthrough. She has transformed internally on some level. To give it a positive meaning for a learning point for future reference, review what just happened in a few brief phrases that are comforting and encouraging. It could be something like, *"Wow baby, that was hard work you just did. I'm so proud of you for letting the yuckies just pass through you instead of holding onto it."* Or, you could say, *"I love you baby. It's OK to feel those big, scary feelings. The best is to let it pass through you just like you did so it doesn't stay inside. Good work."* It lets her know that she is loved, accepted, seen, and everything is OK in her world. As the chapters unfold, we will be taking a closer look at each step.

What is an emotional breakdown anyway? Is it just a child acting insane to drive you crazy? No! Don't take it personally. Don't take anything personal in life. That's the first rule in Don Miguel Ruiz's book, *The Four Agreements*. I highly recommend this mind- opening book capable of transforming your life. Circling back, the child wants nothing more than to be loved and accepted. On the surface, it may appear that the child is pushing your buttons to piss you off. Or it looks like she's weak and unable to control herself. But if you don't give her the tools to authentically process the emotions that all humans experience, what can you expect from her? And what will her life be like as an adult with no emotional intelligence to transform her own challenges in life? Will she become addicted to drugs to numb the pain? Will she be a functional drunk to appear successful, but require a constant stream of alcohol in her blood to drown out the monsters in her mind? Why are we pressuring these innocent young learners with the heavy expectations of the world? Who cares what other people think? Let's put more weight on arming these young people with the tools of emotional and mental mastery. That is true power. Acceptance from the external world is fleeting and a shape-shifting illusion. Self-acceptance internally and a strong connection to the inner presence, which is Source energy, is how we can give these children the gift of true power.

What happens most often is this: the rage and sadness in the child is so raw and uninhibited, it actually triggers the adult into a highly uncomfortable state. The adult can't handle all the authentic darkness exploding into the open air. They weren't allowed to let it out as a child, so the automatic response is to teach their children the same beliefs. The logical reasons to stop the child is to say, "Hey, you're a big kid now. You need to learn to control your emotions." What's really being communicated is, "Hey, you've been alive for 5, 10, or 15 years now and I expect you to suppress your dark emotions because it makes me feel uncomfortable." Another logical reason is to say, "What are other people going to think? You can't act this way!" The unfortunate message delivered is, "You should care more about what other people think than caring about process-ing your frustrations in life." What if we became aware of the unconscious programs we are perpetuating without aware-ness? Now that you see it, I bet you feel a little more aware and have some type of "aha" moment.

Think about this: Whether it's someone you know, or your-self, how many adults do you know who continuously sup-press, repress, and ignore their emotions until they burst at the seams oozing into every area of life? It gets messy, ugly, and sticky. It's so much harder to do the cleanup work when the darkness has been brooding in the closet for all those years. The longer it has had a chance to ferment, the bigger the monster-like qualities it is going to possess. That's because it has had time to morph, collect evidence, and make up more layers of untrue stories to back it up until the thing is so huge, you're terrified to let it out. Add on top of that self-judgment and the fear of what someone else might think, and forget it. It feels totally and completely hopeless! Don't even bother. You're doomed! OK, I'll save the drama here. You see what I'm saying though. When you brush it under the rug or stuff it down into a bottle, it's no *bueno*! You have to deal with it one way or another, sooner or later. It's always better to find the courage to face it head on as soon as you can. You'll strengthen your level of courage and get used to doing it this way until it becomes your natural way of being. If at first, it's too big and scary, that's OK! It's normal. You've been using the same tactic your adults taught you since childhood. You've had a lot of practice doing it that way. When you attempt a new way, at first, it'll seem daunting and unnatural. It might even feel wrong like when you try to cross your arms the other way. Try it right now. I bet you cross your arms with the same arm over the other every time. Now try it the other way around. Can you do it? I can't. It's hard to even get the arms in that position. And when it's there, how does it feel? Totally foreign, right? What is happening there? You've been doing it the same way for all these years that doing it the other way is unfamiliar. The unfamiliarity makes it feel wrong. But is there a wrong way to cross your arms? Of course not! Interesting, right? The neurology in your brain has been accustomed to firing off the same synapses forming a strong neural pathway, therefore you formed a habit. The sneaky thing about a habit is that it feels familiar and comfortable. That familiarity and comfort is what tricks people into thinking doing it the way you've always done it is the *right* way to do it. Did that make sense? It's worth re-reading. It's important to get this point for all the transformational work you'll be doing on yourself in order to be the conscious leader of your family and most importantly for your strong willed and hypersensitive child. She's counting on you to get this in order to lead her through these early learning years. Your child is so fortunate to have a brave mother who is willing to expand herself in order to support her path as an awakened being here to do great things in the world. Thank you for being you. I appreciate your presence and desire to step up to the plate. I've been there and have helped many others go through this process. You can do it, too.

CHAPTER 3

Making Sense of Meltdowns

"You must learn a new way to think
before you can master a new way to be."
–Marianne Williamson

OK, let's talk about why your child is hypersensitive. Do you have any ideas why she's so sensitive? It's not because she's spoiled, coddled, or doing her best to piss you off. What if there is a perfectly spiritual purpose behind it all? The hypersensitive child I'm referring to is the one who is doing her best to be a new person in this world, but is having a hard time. She's a good kid overall; she's loving and wants to be loved. She's learning the ropes to life and you are her main guide. In fact, if you see yourself as her guardian angel, you will catch the energy behind a pivotal idea. Most parents mistakenly think because the child is small that she knows very little. Many adults also think that because they are the older one, then they always know what's best. They expect the child to follow directions simply because they said so. The most empowering position, however, is to be a loving guide at her side, allowing her to find the way best suited for her life plan, like a life coach. What works for one person doesn't always work for the next. This is true no matter the race, age, gender, or spiritual beliefs. Hold the space for her to be her own person as you do your best to show her the way. Even if she falls numerous times on her face, she will be that much stronger when it's time to set her free into the world. This is a practice that requires mega self-awareness. It is a delicate balancing act between sharing what you *think* is best from personal experience and allowing her to find her own way. The reality is this type of space gives her the chance to fail in a loving environment, one that is built on the faith that she is capable of figuring things out. If she seeks your help, you are always there ready to present empowering information for her review. As she experiments with ideas over time, she will eventually develop a set of tools and internal processes that will heighten her level of emotional intelligence.

Emotional intelligence is a power that anyone can develop, if given the opportunity, but few know how to seek. It's paramount in helping you understand yourself, the people in the world around you and how to have meaningful relationships. It's about recognizing your own emotions, those of others and how to manage them all in a way that serves. It requires the use of your discernment to know between the two. Daniel Goleman wrote a book in 1995 with the title, *Emotional Intelligence* (EI), and remains the authority on the subject. The four components of EI are: 1) self-awareness, 2) self-management, 3) social awareness, and 4) relationship management. Top businesses will attest to emotional intelligence as the key ingredient in a powerful leader. This is a learned behavior that few people have the chance to develop unless they actively seek out the training and information. While the book is a study on top business leaders, this applies to all people. For what is a leader? A leader is not only someone at the helm of a nation or a Fortune 500 company. It is the individual person leading a life; it is everyone. A mother practicing conscious parenting is leading herself and her family with an awakened perspective. A father who chooses to buy non-GMO foods in an attempt to avoid harmful ingredients is leading himself and his family in a life-affirming direction. A child learning the boundary between her emotions and another person's is gaining the foundations to wielding the power of emotional intelligence. Gone are the days where skills and intellectual intelligence are enough to succeed in this world. We are all leaders. Unless you recognize that, you will never have the power to harness it. Until you claim your own leadership position, you won't be able to model that for your child. Isn't that ultimately what you want? To raise a child who will have the tools to powerfully live out her full potential and success in all areas of her life? When you walk your talk, she will follow suit.

Interestingly enough, in the same year of 1995, Dr. David Hawkins released a book titled, *Power vs. Force*. Here, he investigated human consciousness and established a scale from 1 to 1,000 charting the calibration of different human emotions. At the low-end, you'll find human experiences like guilt (30), fear (100), and danger (150). These states keep people stuck in victimhood and totally disempowered in life. In those lower vibrational states, people are less able to lead inspiring lives marked by hope, faith, and love. There's no true power there – only the use of force to push one's way through the day to day dramas. As you move up from the 150 calibration of anger to courage at 200, possibilities begin to open up and things can start to shift. This is a turning point. If you can inch your way up little by little, then you may head into willingness (310), reason (400) and love (500). You can use the Law of Attraction, the Sedona Method, and the tools detailed in this book, The Empowered Child, to support your move up the scale. The higher end of the spectrum from 600-1,000 are states of peace and enlightenment. People like Christ, Krishna, and Buddha, who calibrated at 1,000, were able to impact the whole of humanity simply with their way of being on a vibrational level. Dr. Hawkins stated that in 1995, 82 percent of the global population calibrated at 200 and lower. Most people were living a life stuck by fear, anger, and pride. If the majority of the human race was living in the emotional dumps, then the collective consciousness was spilling over with a negative energy impacting the whole world at once.

Why is this important and how does it relate to your child? By having the tools of emotional intelligence and leading a life vibrationally calibrated on the higher end of the spectrum, she will be armed with the tools necessary to lead herself and others into the world we all dream of. Who wants a world marked by peace, collaboration, and abundance? I do! It starts here with you, me, and our children. By waking up to empowering information and having the courage to take immediate right action, we can all rise together. This is how all ships will rise with the tide.

Dr. Bruce Lipton, a cell biologist and author of *The Biology of Belief* teaches how the mind is the instrument that manipulates the body's DNA, not the other way around. This is ground-breaking information. It throws out the old idea that your potential is limited to the genes inherited from your ancestors. It puts the power and responsibility right back to the people. It also means people will have to be courageous enough to use that as an inspiring catalyst rather than hold onto the old crutch due to the fear of change. It's an easy way out of pushing yourself to greatness when you can blame your misfortunes on your genes. His research in epigenetics is impacting university texts today. His discoveries illustrate that by changing your perception, thoughts, and beliefs, your mind can alter the activity of your genes. Through manipulating the environment of the cell- filled petri dishes, he found that *the environment determined the fate of the cells, not the genetic pattern* itself. Basically, you are free to be who you want to be. It all begins in your mind with the type of thoughts you choose to hold. You had the power all along. Although no one taught you before, now your child gets to benefit from this information. It's all in your mind. The quality of the thoughts you hold will become the quality of the experiences you have in life. Training yourself to have the habit of thinking empowering thoughts will bring forth a positive life experience. When you model that, your child will automatically absorb this through osmosis.

Your child is sensitive because she has been brought into the world through an awakened person. I'm willing to bet that you have done some level of self-development work to get yourself to a more conscious state of being. If you are a conscious person, were you always conscious or did you have a defining moment? What was it? Most people had a defining moment that led them to claim the path of conscious living. It was a big moment that kicked your mental jail wide open giving you the taste of true freedom. Once you were free, there was no way you were ever going back. It's like taking the red pill in the Matrix and seeing it all break open. Was your defining moment painful or traumatic? And as soon as you got to the other side, you looked back and said, "Holy moly! I made it through hell, and wow! I see the truth now. I didn't die. I grew." It's as if you were a snake that shed its outer layer, looking back to witness the old you dead on the ground. And now you're grateful to expand into a wiser version of yourself with more insights and awareness in your memory bank. All that work caused you to shift your perspective. This process allowed you to change your beliefs. Changing your beliefs altered your DNA. That genetic upgrade impacted your child's DNA in an empowering way. Now, you have a genetic explanation as to why your child is more awake than the average child.

Here's another incredible story showing the invisible, yet measurable, connection in the physical world. There is so much information that isn't taught and discussed that gives added depth and meaning to life. In 1997, Dr. Nicolas Gisin conducted an experiment to demonstrate how two photons of light seven miles apart were able to simultaneously respond to a stimulus applied to only one of them. They were twin photons separated by a dramatic distance apart, yet remained *in touch no matter the distance*. He was testing a prediction of past quantum physicists that *entangled particles continue to communicate with each other instantaneously even when very far apart*, even across the world. This is an explanation of the uncanny connection between mother and child. It's also a possible reason why your change in DNA through personal development has impacted your child before she was conceived or even after she was born. All of the personal development work you have done in the past and continue to do will greatly impact your child's level of awareness now and for generations to come.

On a spiritual level, these highly sensitive children act out in challenging ways at times because, like a sponge, they are empathically absorbing the negative vibrations blanketing the globe. More than that, they are acting as an energy filtration system for the collective consciousness of the world. What is the collective consciousness? It is an energy created from the beliefs held by the majority of humans. If you want to know what those beliefs are, take a look at the current state of world affairs and the commonality of fear and lacking begin to reveal what's hidden in the minds of most. These children have come to change the world. The negative energy in the world is passing through these children like a filter. They process it unconsciously and benefit the world in that way. Just like how the leaves of a tree transform harmful carbon dioxide into life-giving oxygen, these empathic children are transforming lethal negative vibrations and attuning them to a higher vibration through the instrument of their bodies. Pema Chodron, the Buddhist nun, author, and teacher, talks about meditating in a similar way. She calls it *tonglen*, a practice that leads to compassion and peace in the world. You do this by breathing in all the pains of the world and breathing it out as love and light. It is a great service to humanity when someone practices this type of meditation. Understanding the greater role your child is playing offers a perspective marked by compassion. Remaining in touch with her purpose and service instantly flips the adult's attitude from frustration to gratitude.

Parents using force to get their agendas met add unnecessary pressure to these hyper-sensitive children who are absorbing and processing the emotions and energies of the whole world. Many times, they are silently working out the challenges that their families are experiencing. If the bills can't get paid on time and there is mounting debt, there's stress. If the parents are not in a loving relationship and are living inauthentic lives, that's building up negative energy in the home. If the media shows and conversations circling in their lives are mainly drama and trauma filled, it's dragging the mood down into the dumps. Sensitive children are feeling everyone's feelings, thoughts, and emotions very intensely. Add onto that the adult's use of physical, energetic, or psychological force to make the child comply with their idea of what's acceptable behavior. It's not surprising her energetic coping system will implode or explode. If she hasn't been shown a healthy way to process and let the energy out of her body and space, how will she know? Why is the adult's way the only way? Let her punch a pillow or kick a punching bag. Why not? Let her scream at full force into a pillow. Let her cry her heart out in her room. Give her the freedom to feel the emotions fully because eventually it will pass through her if it is allowed to do so. If she is made wrong for all of this, it will force her to push it down into the depths of her being. It will get stored in her cellular memory until it makes her sick physically, psychologically, emotionally, or spiritually. You must have the courage to allow the scary feelings to come out into the open. If you are deeply uncomfortable holding space and bearing witness to her experience, can you imagine how terrifying these huge feelings must be for a little person who is still learning the ropes to life? You're an adult with decades of experience dealing with emotions. You're able to recognize, label, and effectively manage them. Hopefully, you have the tools to transform and heal them, too. If not, find a coach, like me, who can help. We have training programs teaching parents exactly how to transform themselves so they may better serve their child. Now, it's your turn to coach her through these scary moments. I'll show you how. Many adults still stuff down their emotions, leading to the high rate of heart disease, cancer, strokes, and weight gain. Louise Hay, publisher and author of *Heal Your Body*, spent her life helping people understand how your beliefs can either harm or heal your body. Let's pass the available tools of wisdom down to these spiritually awakened children so they may fulfill their purpose with greater ease and grace. They have come to be the change. We are here to facilitate the journey.

CHAPTER 4

Step 1:
Evaluate the Situation

*"Remind yourself that you cannot fail
at being yourself."*
–Wayne Dyer

C hallenges and conflicts are undoubtedly a part of life. They hold the potential for emotional growth, conscious expansion, and the journey toward spiritual maturity. If there is no room in your life for difficult moments, when it happens you will be totally shattered. Managing your expectations and steering clear of perfectionism will set you on the path with greater ease. You and your child's ability to harvest these potential moments depend on each person's attitude and perception. Your attitudes and perceptions are created by the subconscious beliefs you hold in your mind. Your beliefs were created earlier on in life during the childhood years. This brings it full circle. Your childhood beliefs, stored in your subconscious mind, directly impact the way you view the world and how you show up as a mom. This, in turn, plants the seeds of beliefs in your child's subconscious mind, which will directly impact the way she views the world and shows up as a woman. This cycle has been happening through the ages all the way up your ancestral lineage and it will continue to pass. You get to have the choice as to what kind of impact you want to pass on to future generations in the present moment.

When your child is having a hard time, first evaluate the situation. Diagnose the situation like a doctor and eliminate possible causes for the upset. Imagine you have a checklist in your mind. Assess the body from an external perspective to find out if she's injured or hurt. Her system could be hungry and getting increasingly moody. Has she eaten in the last two hours and is in the middle of a growth spurt? From an emotional standpoint, think about whether she's had any interactions with friends and family that might have caused a perceived hurt in her feelings and self-image. If her mind is negatively focused, she will experience a downward spiral in her emotions. Did she hear or watch something too advanced for her age, which is causing fear and uncertainty? Does she have pent-up emotions from little hurts here and there that need acknowledging? Her spirit could be crying out for help. These are the mind, body, and spirit aspects to consider. Then, there's also all the various roles she plays and relationships she needs to think about, too. Once you are armed with the information and gain greater awareness into the root of the issue, then you can communicate to that pain point with increased effectiveness. Life is a deep subject filled with infinite mysteries and eternal truths. What goes on externally in the day to day operations of the family routine, work, and relationships are an extension of your internal environment.

Perhaps your child is spiritually gifted. There are many labels out there referring to the influx of enlightened children here to do great work. The different generations were given names like Rainbow, Indigo, Crystal, and Starseed all with their own list of characteristics describing the dominant color in their aura or the galactic information seeded within them to bring waves of light to this world. These highly-gifted children are sensitive in different ways. On the one hand, they are sensitive psychically, intuitively, and energetically. They are in touch and naturally more developed with various spiritual gifts, like telekinesis, teleportation, telepathy, and more. They may readily access their ability to know, see, hear, and feel information through their extra sensory capabilities. On another hand, they are also hyper sensitive and deeply agitated by loud volume, bright lights, excess temperatures, fabric seams, clothing tags, and certain social interactions accepted by the masses. For example, touching or entering a hyper- sensitive child's space without building rapport or forming trust can instantly send her into hysterics. She feels threatened and is acting out with the only reaction she knows at that time to express her overwhelming fear. It is a defense mechanism. She is sensing something about the situation that her adult isn't. Therefore, honoring her ability to read a scenario and politely acting as her voice and bodyguard in those early years are extremely beneficial to supporting her skills and abilities. Compare that to a parent who, with great intentions, perceiving the world through her own lens of what's good and bad, constantly overrides the scene and tells the child exactly what to think and do. Either the child will not comply and be viewed as strong willed, or the child will eventually learn to ignore her inner cues and lose touch with her innate abilities. Worse, she will lose touch with her internal GPS, her intuition. Evaluate if there is someone or something in the vicinity that is freaking her out on an energetic level. For a highly sensitive person, she is very present to energy and how it impacts her on all levels.

Each enlightened generation came serving what was most needed at the time. Earlier waves came to carve out the path in a highly-unconscious world. They needed very strong warrior traits to fight the big fight. Newer generations are being the change and leading the way by modeling and teaching the tools of light, compassion, unconditional love, collaboration, and empathy. While it is true that these numerous waves of awakened children came forth to serve humanity, I also believe that all people are born with the wisdom and light embedded within them. We are all powerful. Whether you experience a powerful life depends on the programs and beliefs you allow to run in your mind. Installing empowering programs in your children now will shorten their path to knowing the truth of who they really are. It is only by remembering who you really are that you can reclaim that power and leadership position. What beliefs are you programming? Are some of the challenges stemming from a need for more empowering beliefs?

To be awake is a gift. It takes growth, courage, and persistence to keep expanding to greater heights. When you are this person, your child has an incredible opportunity to come into this dimension and stay awake. The luckiest child is the one who is born into a conscious family. A tremendous amount of groundwork has been laid to provide an awakened environment for her to come into. Rather than start from scratch during the learning curve of life, she has guides who are able to protect her from the illusory ways and hold the path open to a life guided by light and truth. From a soul level, she also had a part in choosing the family she would be born into. She chose this unit because it was a clearer path to fulfilling her purpose.

Many times, for you to lead an awakened life, you had to break away from your family's beliefs and practices. You were often seen as the black sheep, someone who was weird and didn't quite fit in. Your loved ones gave you a hard time for not following the rules. They judged, shamed, and pointed the finger at you for too many reasons. Well, good for you! That meant you had the guts to follow your intuition and used your discernment to feel into each moment. You had the courage to use your senses to determine if something was true or false. You trusted your heart to sense whether something felt off or in alignment with your truth. Living life based on rote tradition is empty and without meaning. It is the cause behind many prejudices and wars. Carving out your own path is the only way to real freedom.

If you weren't the ceremonial black sheep, then someone in the lineage before you had to bear the badge of honor. She was the pioneer who chopped down a path in the forest in honor of the ones to come after her. You were passed the baton to keep the mission alive. Now you have been gifted another life in this line of awakened beings to one day run into the world holding the torch overhead leading the charge to a greater light-filled reality. From this understanding and acceptance of a greater mission, clarity flows in with ease and grace. You and your child have come for a great purpose.

The collective human race is currently acting like it has gone totally mad. There are wars that never end, causing cascades of heartache and pain. Laws and regulations are suppressing the freedom of choice and leading to an uprise of angry citizens. The food and water distributed are imposters' products filled with poison. Medical practices and the pharmaceutical industry are actively serving a money trail more than saving lives. There is a heightened sense of negativity and drama being played out across the board. People are being controlled by falling into traps designed to create fear. Many plans are created to keep the people sick, in debt, disempowered, and living in a low vibrational state day in and day out. This further gets perpetuated into future generations from stories of personal struggle and never getting ahead. Then, the tradition of that belief continues as it gets planted into the mind of the young. How much does that play into the times when your child has a really tough day and triggers a negative dynamic? NO! Stop the insanity! You can stop it and so can everyone else who finds the courage to break free from the limiting beliefs running in their subconscious minds. It requires courage, awareness, and persistence. It requires bravery, faith, and trust. It requires vision, empowerment, and inspiration. How much longer do you want to be part of the equation that perpetuates the tradition of fear in your lineage? Most people don't even know they are part of the equation. That fact alone keeps them in the dark, powerless and incapable of change. The ones who get a glimpse but have no support might fall back into the old ways because it is just too scary to take on the world by oneself. Know that you are not alone. All across the world people are waking up in rapid succession. They are waking up to their innate spiritual gifts. They are waking up to the light and truth seeded within them. Stay conscious. Surround yourself with like-minded people willing to empower each other to elevate every moment of every day. How would having an empowered community make a difference in your child's life?

People are being made physically sick so the state of fear can be extended. Once you adopt the lifestyle of transforming struggle into empowerment, then you become the queen of your realm, able to break free from the loop of hopelessness. The cycle stops here. The cycle ends with you. Generation after generation of unconscious living will no longer be the tradition. Humanity is beginning to wake up from the hypnotic slumber of fear and illusions. When each individual crosses to the side of awakened living, then the collective human race will rise and elevate itself vibrationally as a whole.

Children who are fortunate enough to be born into a family that has done the groundwork of being awake get the opportunity to remain conscious to who they are and why they are here. We are alive in very exciting times. The pendulum swings as far to the right as is does to the left, in equal proportions. Our world is experiencing an intense swing into one end of the spectrum and feeling the shift from one end to the other. Everything in the world seems crazy, insane, and chaotic. Nothing makes sense and systems are breaking down in multiple sectors. This is good news! Stay steady and rooted in truth. For the collective race of humanity to swing from unconscious living to conscious living, all the fears that have been suppressed for centuries must come up for healing, reconciliation, and release. What has once been hiding in the shadow side of ourselves and the collective are surfacing to the light of day to be transformed. Is that collective vibration bombarding your child's energetic body causing her to shut down?

These hypersensitive and strong-willed children are often empaths, people who absorb energy from the people around them, and even from the world at large. It is not bound by space and time. Empaths are able to tune in and feel into a situation or person all the way across the globe. They are sensitive to the energies that float in the ethers. These types of people often show psychic ability. The challenge is many don't have the chance to learn how to fully use it to their advantage. Most don't even know they have this ability. They just think they're really good at reading people, body language, or facial expressions. They believe they're simply great at being in tune with people or great at building rapport. It can be really easy to get along with people sometimes because empaths are able to instantly know how someone feels. Other times, it may be impossible to get along with another person because they are absorbing all their negative energies and subconsciously protecting themselves by moving their bodies away or closing themselves off from personal interactions. Without mastery, empaths often fall prey to other people's moods and soak them in as their own, like a sponge. It all happens without effort and often without awareness. This is when it gets tricky and draining. When you don't realize you've taken on someone else's negative energy as your own, you lack the power to shift out of that state. When your child is not acting like her usual self, take a moment to sense whether she's taken on other people's energies.

These children have come to be the change. You and I are here to hold the path of consciousness open for them so they may benefit from the work we've already done. Teach them the tools of self-mastery, expanding consciousness and tools to empower them to safely be their full selves. Empaths who don't know how to hold a healthy boundary with the world around them can often get ill or be overwhelmed and become reclusive as a preventative measure. They don't know how to define where their energy ends and another person's energy begins. They can lack the skills to stand confidently and assert their own thoughts, ideas, and existence. This is very disempowering for someone who came here with a great mission to accomplish. That's why one of the biggest emphases to make is the importance of teaching these highly sensitive people how to wield their power. What may seem like a curse to someone without the training is a superpower to one who has been trained and continues to learn. Your child has come through you for a specific purpose and mission. You accepted this relationship long before she was born. Before each physical incarnation, every soul will choose the lessons it wants to experience, who to learn them with and what roles each soul will play. Most likely, you have already known each other before and traveled through many lifetimes together. Sometimes you're the mom; sometimes she's the mom. And the roles can change very drastically to fulfill whatever plan was created before anyone was born into human form. In that realm, there is no right or wrong, good or bad. It's all love. Everything is play on Earth school. Even the person who hurt you the deepest agreed to play the baddest villain in your life in order to help you learn whatever you chose for this incarnation. In fact, the one who played the bad guy in this life loved you so much as a soul that he agreed to risk you hating them. Check out the book, *The Little Soul and the Sun* by Neale Donald Walsch. He has a beautiful way of telling that truth through a children's story. Without the bad guy there to trigger your pain to the surface, you could never heal and evolve into the amazing person you are today.

You and your child agreed to these roles before either of you were born this time around. She agreed to be a powerful soul leader in human form here to be a positive influence in this world. You agreed to facilitate this journey by doing the work to be awake, too. Now is the time we awaken this contract and get to work. Part of your role includes the important first step of evaluating each challenging situation from a diagnostic point of view. I am so proud of you for being conscious and aware. I am grateful you are willing, able, and inspired. You are a divine being created in the image and likeness of the universal Source energy. It is the greater intelligence that breathes life into all things – the greater being that is unnamable and ineffable. You and I are both an extension of this greater Source energy. For that reason, I can say I love and appreciate you. We are connected, we are united. Let's do this! Let's get you and your child the tools to empower yourselves to an elevated vibration. You are powerful. Together, we are unstoppable.

CHAPTER 5

Step 2:
Make Yourself Available

"Who would you be without your story?"
–Byron Katie

When your child is in the midst of an emotional challenge, realize that whatever level of discomfort you may be feeling, it's many times harder for a little person learning how to be in this world. Making yourself available by being fully present in this moment with her is the best thing you can do. Whether she is two or 15, there are always emotionally challenging scenarios that a loving adult can help shed light onto. Think about you or your friend. Even adults have these challenges, right? It's not about not having them, it's about having the tools and consciousness to navigate through them with added ease and grace. It's also about filtering for the lessons so something beneficial can come out of it.

Once you've taken Step 1 to evaluate the situation and establish whether it is an acute cause, like falling, or an accumulated cause, like months of buried emotions, you are better positioned to guide her through the momentary darkness. Step 2 is to make yourself totally available to your child. What does this mean? Turn off the television and music. Mute your cell phone. Turn off the stove. Eliminate all distractions as if this were your one and only client in the world. What's needed here is your full presence as you channel an increased level of unconditional love to the situation.

There is an epidemic right now where a deadly virus has infected the majority of the globe. This sickness causes people to look functional, but they are actually zombies in a deep hypnotic trance. They are asleep at the wheel and no one is directing their lives with conscious awareness. This leaves them disempowered and susceptible to being controlled by mass consciousness. Worse than that, it makes them totally unavailable to creating their best lives or be fully present to their children. Physically, the bodies look well, but in their work, relationships, and health, the stench of decay is exposing the truth. The life force within is disintegrating and no one is paying attention because the external world is a master of distractions. The entertaining show of smoke and mirrors easily keeps the zombies asleep in the driver's seat. Who's driving then? People are unjustly bombarded with massive levels of delusional propaganda, handed out like candy through everything they come in contact with: television, news, movies, magazines, textbooks, schools, government, religion, ancestral stories, food, medicine, and even the air. The programs you buy into are the life experience you will have. It's a direct correlation. What you tune into and pay attention to is the reality you experience. The more doom and gloom you allow into your space, the more you are creating in like-kind. Everyone is powerfully creating all the time. It's a matter of whether you are doing it with purpose to reach your goals or without intention and keeping yourself stuck in limbo.

Gladly, you are not a zombie. How did you overcome your hypnotic state? How did you wake up from your trance? This was no small feat. This was the defining moment that caused you to snap out of a drug-like coma and discover the stark difference between living unconsciously in the dark and consciously in the light. As you go further on this path of enlightenment, one where you continuously follow the light of truth, you will find expanded freedom. This freedom comes from the reconnection with who you really are, a soul in human form. The more time you spend each day communing with your inner self, the intangible spirit within you that never dies, the more you own your true power. The more you dive into this sacred space the more you establish the empowering line of contact between you and your personal energy Source. Your ability to know and act for the highest good increases with ease and grace. It takes practice. You must put in the committed effort day after day. Soon you will see, feel, and know the impact of taking little steps each day toward an empowered life. What if all children had the chance to keep this conscious connection alive from birth? What if you were the one who exercised full presence to coach your child through this journey? How much more powerful could she be?

As soon as your soul came into formation, it became an eternal entity, as energy is never created nor destroyed – it only gets transformed. This is true for every soul. Imagine a great big light source in the shape of a ball. Coming off this huge round ball of light are tons of thin straight filaments with tiny balls at the ends. These filaments are like fiber optics where it can transfer the main source of light all the way down to the tiny balls on the other end. That tiny ball holds the same light as the source light. As you zoom out from this picture, you see there are billions of these thin filaments with tiny balls at the ends. This is how I imagine Source creative energy that breathes life into all things and the billions of people that hold the same light. Everyone has this light shining within. You were born with it. The difference in one's life experience and ability to live one's soul purpose, a.k.a. dharma, is the level of awareness a person exercises.

Some of these balls at the end of the filament, although they contain the light of Source at its core, appear largely dimmed and almost without their natural glow. What's happening there? The light within has not altered. It has fallen into the trap of delusion causing its outer surface to hold numerous layers of false beliefs. The lies and illusions cover up the light emanating continuously from within. The tiny ball is your body. The light within is your soul shining the light of Source. The light is a constant. There is no effort in having the light, it simply is. The layers of false beliefs are like blackout curtains blocking out the light. These false beliefs are things like feeling inferior, fear of failure, fear of success, fear of change, fear of things that are different, fear of shining, fear of being authentic, fear of not being liked, and on and on. The blackout layers can also be unhealed trauma that attracts dramatic situations to complain about in order to perpetuate the undigested pain beneath the surface. There are many variations of what fear morphs into. Your daily task is to practice hawk-like awareness and transform the slightest hint of fear. If you are to live your life to the fullest, you must be in your power position perched up high to gain an expansive perspective.

Often the daily drama of life insidiously draws you in, away from that powerful position of expanded awareness. That is the same way it pulls you out of the present moment. To worry about the past or the future allows the content of the stories to distract you from the powerful moment of the now. The drama lures you in until it becomes the main point of focus. Imagine drawing a small dot on a piece of paper. Now, hold the paper up to your nose so all you can see is this paper and maybe a blurry dot. This is a stance outside of the power position. No longer do you possess the ability to see with clarity. It can happen without detection if self-awareness isn't turned on. At first, it shows up as venting to a trusted friend because it's been a stressful week. Then, it turns into complaining to every person who will listen. Before you know it, your life seems to give you more unbelievable things to complain about and the downward spiral is in full force. Ask yourself in these moments and during the times when your child is going through her own emotional challenge: *Is complaining and thinking thoughts of frustration really serving you and the situation?* This is the law of attraction at work. Emotions are vibrational and attract in like-kind. No worries!! Simply notice when it happens, then have the courage to take immediate right action and love yourself through the process. We are not shooting for perfection. We are aiming for a conscious daily practice. Immediate right action is this: 1) Stop without self-judgment; 2) Take a deep breath; 3) Love yourself unconditionally; 4) Pivot your thoughts upward. *Reach for the next better feeling thought*, as Abraham-Hicks often says in the Law of Attraction teachings. You don't have to hop from the first step to the twentieth step. Just take the next baby step, then repeat over time. When you coach yourself through challenging times, you become more available as a guide to your child. Leading yourself upward requires your active participation and mental awareness of what you're thinking and how you're being. Your evolution allows you to be more fully present and accessible to support your child in times of need. Her emotional outbursts are less likely to trigger an undigested wound in you. Instead, you will have the calmness of an unattached mom being capable of leading her through the storm. This is powerful. In the early years, you are leading her. Later on, she will internalize the process and be able to lead herself. It all begins with your personal practice so you may be available to her needs.

Fear does have an important role in life. It keeps your body out of harm's way. It tells you not to touch the fire or cross the street when a huge truck is speeding by. It has a purpose, for sure. It gets in the way, however, when it thinks everything is going to kill you. Without a threat to your survival, it's out of a job! So, it does what it does best. It will fabricate mental blocks that bleed into psychological, emotional, physical, relationship, or money issues. It creates drama so it can swoop in as the hero to keep you alive. When standing up and speaking your truth is so embarrassing you feel like dying, then your ego will come to the rescue and hold you back from ever doing it again. Why is this a problem? All the way from the boardroom to the family room, if you are unable to speak your truth authentically, you will be giving your power away and feel powerless as a result. This impacts your ability to truly lead your child. First, it will be challenging to maintain healthy boundaries with your child. Your voice is your power. If you cannot communicate what is acceptable and unacceptable, or what is safe or unsafe, the boundaries are wishy-washy. If the boundaries are unstable, your child will not know what to trust, nor will she feel safe. Second, if you do not cultivate yourself to have the power of your voice, that disempowering message will be unconsciously transmitted to your child on a vibratory level and through physical modeling. Being able to communicate your truth from a place of love in every situation renders you effective and powerful. This is the message to instill in your child from the start. Many people have to face this fear later in life and it holds them back from living their full life. This fear exists because the mind is consumed by the unconscious limiting beliefs that are clamoring for its attention. It is pulling you out of the now making you less available to the present moment.

This misguided focus causes unhappiness as your inner self knows that you are not being true to your soul's purpose. Emotional discomforts are messages from your inner self letting you know you are way off course. It has to find a way to communicate with your mind and body in order to gain congruency and alignment. When the mind and body are off doing their own thing as programmed from the outer world and following what the ego personality is dictating as life or death situations, the soul has to wait patiently and find some way to communicate with you. Negative emotions are one modality of communication it will use to get your attention. When you find yourself crying for days on end, or at inopportune times, eventually you might stop and question, "What the heck is happening?" You might finally reach a breaking point and ponder it enough to ask the universe the right questions. When you ask the universe a question, prepare to hear the answer. It might not come immediately, but if you pay attention in all the ways you can develop your sensory abilities, eventually you will pick up on the answer.

Another tactic your inner self will communicate with you is the type of experiences you have in life. Anytime you notice a negative pattern or repetitive story you are sick of going through, this is a tip-off that there is a huge cosmic message blinking in your direction. First, the message comes as a pebble thrown in your path. If you're too busy and go about your way, the next message will be a rock thrown at your feet. Then, a brick. Then a cinder block. This goes on until eventually you get a boulder thrown at your head. This time you get knocked over and you throw your hands in the air exclaiming, "Why me?" If that happens, listen up! Life is talking to you. It's telling you to pay attention to the signs. There are signs everywhere all the time. The catch is, you've got to stay present and be aware. This is what allows you to be available to life and keeps you open to your child. When you are fully present, the amount of coincidences increases and quickly turns into daily synchronistic events. Keep this up and soon it becomes so commonplace your life is filled with magic. It's true! Every conversation you overhear, every billboard you see, every song you hear will be speaking straight to you. Then, a daily dose of gratitude rushes over you because you understand the universal current of love is flowing through everyone, everything, and everywhere, including you. It brings you a sense of peace, safety, and wellness. This is a sure sign that you've been diligently practicing your path and are enjoying the alignment between your soul, mind, and body. If you can hand over the keys of life to your Source energy, then you have effectively gotten out of your own way. When you get to this point of handing yourself over to the greater power, you've already been cultivating a deep spiritual practice to make it possible. Congratulations! This means you've been consciously and unconsciously showing your child exactly how to get to this same place of enlightened living. If you can pass the driving wheel of your mind and body to your inner presence, you will love the abundant flow that continuously, easily, and effortlessly pours through you. It's divine, delicious, delectable. It's bliss! This is what every child deserves to learn from the beginning. Correction. They already have this connection. It is our job to keep that line of communication open, rather than shut down from worldly expectations and unconscious programming.

The more you strengthen your connection to Source, the clearer you will be on your life purpose. Before coming into this human incarnation, you and every soul chose the lessons it wanted to experience. You, as a soul, consciously chose a specific mission and purpose to fulfill in this lifetime. You likely had lifetimes before and have infinitely more into the future. Each time, before you returned here with a different name, body, and set of experiences to have, you had the chance to sit with your spiritual guides and mentors to review how it went last time, what you want to do next time, and who you want to play these different roles with. You usually stay within the same soul group while each soul takes turns playing different roles, such as the lover, child, bad guy, or parent. These roles are contracts that both parties agree to. Every situation as a human is co-created between you and Source, and also between you and all the parties involved, long before you materialized physically. Knowing there is a reason for every person we cross paths with and a purpose behind every interaction brings a sense of comfort. There is meaning behind the daily unfolding of life. You aren't here just to push papers at a job you abhor. You didn't come here to wander aimlessly in life. Look at nature. Nothing in nature questions how it fits into the grand scheme of life. It unfolds effortlessly and grows in the flow. It doesn't question the intelligence that is programmed within it. It simply lives and expands. When you start to lose sight, go into nature and witness the abundance and wisdom everywhere around you. It will heal you and get you back in alignment with the divinity that you are. Sit under a tree, breathe fresh air, pay attention to all of the little details and nuances in color and shape. Notice how the light is reflecting off the bit of moisture on the blade of grass in front of you. Getting into this zone of awareness pulls you further into the magic of the present moment. This is something you can easily do with your child on a regular basis. It won't take very long before both of you will be consumed by the beauty and majesty life.

Our children are born wise, awake, and aware. They already know who they are and what they are here for. They are full of hope and light. It is our job and duty to protect that wisdom for them. Adults came here to carve the initial path out for them. We came with the ability to see the truth. Armed with determination and grit, we were fit to take the path less traveled. Before we pass the baton to the next generation, there is a bit of knowledge transfer to smooth the transition. We must realize that we are claiming the vision for their future. You want a safe and thriving Earth for your children to do the same in. You want her to be abundant and full of life. Why is it that adults grow up to be so serious and drained of life? They say it's because there are responsibilities and bills to pay. I disagree. That notion is simply a limiting belief that we can eliminate with a few good tools. You can be happy, fulfilled AND pay your bills. It boils down to whether you have limiting beliefs dictating how you perceive the world to operate. If the beliefs are not serving your highest good of expansion, abundance, and grace, then it is pulling you into fear and worry. Fear and worry causes you to fall out of alignment with the present moment, which knocks you off the empowered position of creating with power and purpose. It further keeps you unavailable to your child in her moments of need. This is the time to bring yourself back to center. Ask yourself, "Am I present in this moment? What am I worried about? What is my mind thinking that is making me stuck in time somewhere else?" Then gently guide yourself back to this place and time where your child is right in front of you. Ahhh...it's a practice. This is precisely the reason the daily meditative practice of bringing the mind back to the breath and Source is infinitely powerful.

Our kids need us to stand strong in the light of truth for them by holding back the expectations of worldly illusions. They came here to do great things. They came here with the light in their eyes and the fire ablaze in their hearts ready to spread love across the globe. They don't have all the layers of gunk adults have blocking out the light. Too many people are still suffering in their own versions of hell. That hell exists only in their minds created by the thoughts and beliefs they've bought into. It is fully possible to transform it, shatter that hell, and create a personal version of heaven. I've done it and have helped many others do it. You can do it, too. These children are born with heaven inside them and they can teach us all about it, as long as we listen and not impose on them the system that was ingrained in us long ago.

The system is like a heavy, invisible net that holds you down. It keeps generations and nations under its control so that your life force energy is wasted in a never-ending cycle of useless drama and repetitive fear-based actions. It's heavy and intended to keep you stuck, if you let it. It keeps humans unaware of the power of aligning with their inner selves. What is the system? It's what we've been discussing all along. The disempowering messages and programs that are infused into everything we come in contact with. It's the method in which people are kept unconscious and out of their power position. It's the way that holds people in a hypnotic state, repeating what has always been done, living an ongoing cycle of birth, school, work, save, retire, hope to travel, and enjoy life finally, then die. It's the collective story of what success is supposed to look like, but look around, how's it working out? It's time to question everything. It's time to carve out your own path of reality. When you do, you are demonstrating the necessary tools of bravery and courage that your child will need to follow suit. It shows what and how to be aware of your own thoughts, how to use your intuition and critical thinking skills like discernment.

You're reading this book because you have been led here on a higher level. There are no accidents. Because we have been guided to be together for a higher purpose, I want to empower you with all you need in order to stand up tall and shine your light. I am doing this to empower your child's journey down her path, as well. Our future generations are counting on us. I am here to support you as you courageously accept your heightened leadership position in your life and in your awakened child's life. She needs you. She picked you because she knew you would be her guardian angel on Earth. She knew you were able and willing to be her energetic body-guard and teacher during her younger human years. She knew you would understand, accept, and champion her abilities. She knew you wouldn't be afraid of what she was capable of doing, nor would you cower due to what the outside world demanded. She knew you were the light tower, the light warrior, the fierce angel that would protect her path while she made her way into the world. This is why she picked you. Before you came into human form, you both agreed to this partnership, this sacred relationship. You knew you were up for the task and so you came. Now you are here, awake and aware, available to fulfill your mission and purpose. Together you are a team, along with the others you've identified, here to make a difference in this fear-dominated world. You see the vision for a love led existence as the norm for all. You hold the belief of a world that is here for the good of all. I believe that, too. I especially believe in you.

As a soul, you chose soul lessons for the purpose of expanding your repertoire of experiences. When a soul incarnates into human form, it forgets who it really is. This is called the veil. As a human who doesn't remember itself as an all-powerful divine creator, these previously chosen soul lessons appear as challenges. These challenges are really hard and can affect you emotionally, psychologically, physically, or in any combination of these. The challenge exists in order for the human to eventually reach deep down within to pull out a hidden resource it had all along. In the very moment you discover your power, you suddenly expanded right there on the spot. This is why they say, "*If it doesn't kill you, it makes you stronger.*" You had to do something you've never done and be someone you've never been before. This is the process of becoming. Therefore, within every situation is planted the enlightening lessons available for all people involved. Your lesson is not connected to anyone else's lessons, even though it sprouted from the same scenario. So, take what's there for you and leave the rest for someone else. When you have the ability to stop yourself in the middle of a conflict and rise up into the sky to look down from a soul level perspective, the emotionality and drama falls away. It takes consistent effort. With intentional practice, you can master this. As you master this, your child is learning through observation.

First, you must have a meditation practice for at least 15 minutes a day. More is better, but 15 minutes is totally doable and extremely beneficial. If you are trying it out for the first time, start with two minutes of quiet time focused on deep relaxing breaths. Then inch you way up minute by minute each day you practice. Next, as soon as you notice a negative emotion or catch yourself in the middle of a conflict, immediately stop. There's no need to judge yourself or the other person. You co-created this, remember? If it's a highly charged situation, then recall that the soul who agreed to play the biggest villain in your life actually did it out of love for you. That soul loved you so much it wanted to help you have the experience you chose. Without the villain, you would not be able to have your chosen lesson. Without your lesson, you would not be able to dig deep to find the hidden power you had all along to overcome such darkness and pain. Without that you could not expand into more of who you really are, a powerful divine being. That's what you designed those experiences to do, to expand your awareness of your inner self. So, in fact, after you get your lesson and pick yourself back up again, please release that bad guy. Let her off the hook from holding the key to your joy or sadness. When you let her go, you reclaim a piece of the power you gave away. The power was always in your hands. Wield that power girl! It all starts with the practice of staying present through meditation, then bringing that into your daily life.

When teaching meditation to your child, you can begin with a smaller number of minutes before increasing over time. Let her be the one to decide how long or short she wants to participate, if at all. She is allowed to change her mind at any time. There are a few fun ways you can do this: 1) Light a candle and put it between the two of you. Then, tell her you want to see who can sit there the longest without moving or talking. All you're going to do is sit there quietly and observe the flame. Blinking is allowed. 2) Go into nature and find a cozy place to sit. As you're sitting side by side, tell her to pick a spot on a tree or flower to look at as you hang out in your natural surroundings. It doesn't have to be strict and regimented. Keep it light and easy. These are a couple fun, open eye meditations. 3) Consider doing a walking meditation. Again, go into nature for a intentionally slow stroll. You're going to be silent for a set amount of time and not make direct eye contact. Ask her to pay attention to the details, like seeing a bug or a little blade of grass. As she notices these little things, ask her to think of reasons why she's grateful for it. For example, noticing a butterfly camouflaged in the bushes makes me feel grateful for its beauty and splendor. Having regular contact with this type of practice is laying the foundations for her to create this self-empowering habit in the future. You are gifting her the power of being available to her life.

When you're at the peak of the challenge, know that your breakthrough is only around the corner. It is right there within sight. That's when you're sweating, shaking, and falling apart. Hold steady and breathe deeply to help move the energy through your body and space. These are the same symptoms a child will experience, too. Take salt water baths with empowering essential oils like frankincense. Get a massage. Spend time in nature. All that you do in an effort to expand your consciousness models vibrationally and situationally to your child that this is the way to true freedom and empowerment. Surround yourself with others on the path and allow support to envelop you. We have a group you can join online to find others in your area. All information will be listed at the end of the book.

As you stride forward spiritually in leaps and bounds, you will increasingly feel the light and truth reprogram every cell of your body. As you do this work, your child will benefit in every way. Teach her what you know; every moment is a teaching moment. When she asks why you are breathing heavily, you can explain that you are using the breath to consciously push the energy of sad feelings or frustration through and out of your body. If you sit with your emotions and breathe it out, you'll notice how it moves. As TCM indicates, emotions are literally energy that flow in and out of your body. When people hold onto energy, it causes dis-ease. When emotions are not allowed to flow through, it causes suffering in the mind, body, and spirit. There are many reasons people grasp with a tight grip. The choice is always available to let go and be witness from a soul level distance filtering for the higher lesson.

As a young person learning the ropes to life on Earth, we must teach them all that we know, then continue to expand our knowledge and wisdom. To talk to your child with this soul level awareness is to offer them an immediate opening to the path of conscious living while on this plane. To show them how easy it is to practice and stay awake, they have the privilege of inheriting heaven on Earth with greater ease. The more children she grows up with in this shared wisdom, the more power she will possess synergistically in being a force for good in this world. The knowledge transfer includes showing her how to be in this world without being of the world. If we can keep the starlit eyes glistening through her lifetime, her presence alone can remind others of their divine inner presence, too. The more people who remember this true aspect of themselves, the greater chances of elevating the global experience as a whole. It all circles back to you as the powerful entity guiding her during these beginning years. To lead others, you must first lead yourself. As you increase your consciousness quotient, she will benefit for her lifetime and then pass it onto the generations ahead. It begins with you and your presence to the moment. Regularly ask yourself, "Am I here now? Or am I worried about something in the past and future?" Then lovingly bring yourself back to center, right here, right now.

CHAPTER 6

Step 3:
Put on Your Coaching Hat

"My presence is my power."
–Gabrielle Bernstein

In this chapter, you're going to see the value of claiming your role as a leader in your life and especially in your child's life. You get to be her empowerment life coach! How cool is that? Did you know that when a tuning fork is already vibrating and a second one is introduced, it will naturally tune to the same frequency as the first one? You are that first tuning fork. The more you elevate your consciousness through internal self-development, the higher you vibrate. You then become the tuning fork to which all other members in your household will tune to. As everyone tunes to this higher frequency and goes into the world, each individual gets to be that tuning fork in the circles that they touch upon. This seemingly subtle force is the power of your presence. When you are aware of your leadership position as her coach, then you become readily available to lead her with greater ease.

Your child may be around the age of a kindergartener, but learning energy management is empowering for everyone. How do you teach your child to recognize where her energy ends and where another person's begins? Not only is this a pillar in developing high emotional intelligence for future success as an entrepreneur, also it is an integral part of enjoying a well-balanced, nurtured, and healthy life in every area. Relationships require energy. Relating with yourself requires energy management, as does, building a business, and taking care of a family. Finally, just being alive requires energy on the most basic molecular level. Learning to know what energy feels like so you may harness it to your advantage is one of the greatest tools a child can receive. Unconditional love, nurturance, and respect come first of course.

Have you ever hung out with someone and after a while you start to feel exhausted and drained? Or have you ever gotten together with a great friend and later felt totally rejuvenated? What's the difference? Let's take a closer look at that. When you look at someone, the first thing most people notice is the physical body, yet there is so much more than meets the eye. Your body consists of a spoonful of atoms vibrating at such a high rate it looks and feels solid. Without the vibrational energy, we would fall into a tiny pile of atoms. When scientists examine gases, liquids, and solids, they identify the wide range of vibrational rates atoms are moving at to produce those varying states of density. While your physical body is dense, internally on a chi or life force level, there is an invisible intangible energy that courses through all that you do and all that you are. With training, this energy is highly palpable and visible. To the untrained, the energetic exchange between bodies will impact you, but you won't understand why you feel drained and moody, or energized and uplifted. Right now, she might not understand the variables that impact how she feels. Imagine how much safer and powerful your child will be once she learns to harness this power? You get to be the one to show her the way.

First, come with me and put on your magic viewing glasses that allow you to see energy. Now, take a look at a human body and find that there are seven energetic layers enveloping the tangible body. These are called the seven subtle bodies. Moving from the physical body outward, the levels become lighter the further out you go. From densest to lightest, you'll find the etheric, emotional, mental, astral, etheric template, celestial, and ketheric template bodies. When working with a child, you can simplify it by calling it one big energy bubble or force field. Everyone has an energy field around them whether or not they intentionally call it into place. It emanates from within us and is impacted by numerous things. For instance, someone who is sick with a serious illness will have this registered on their energetic field. To an intuitive healer, this illness is visible to their inner vision and palpable to their senses. People who are deceptive and break their integrity regularly will hold that vibration in their emanation. Since all people are born with an innate ability to sense energy, as you are an energy being, even the untrained person will feel repelled if being honest and truthful is valued in their life. Others who subscribe to the lower energy field of cheating and stealing, however, might feel compelled and drawn to that same person. Someone who hangs out with people of lower vibration and isn't protective over her energy will begin to calibrate down to be in sync with the people she spends the most amount of time and energy with. So much happens on an invisible level. The good news is you are in control of this and you can show your child how to do this, too.

Dr. Masaro Emoto, a Japanese scientist, studied water in a most profound way. He froze water and took zoomed in pictures of the water crystals. Before taking the photos, he wanted to see whether exposing the water to loving or hurtful words would impact the type of crystals formed. Sometimes he would say the words. Other times he would show the words. He experimented with different languages, and the results were astoundingly consistent. Nurturing words and phrases like, "Thank you" would produce beautiful and mostly symmetrical shapes. Harmful words like "hate" would not be able to produce any crystalline shape. It would be a blob-like substance that had no shape. He extended the experiment to expose the water to classical music or music with depressing lyrics. The results were similar. This tangible evidence shows the vibrational impact words, thoughts, music, objects, and intentions have on matter. If humans and the Earth are made up of more than 70 percent water, then this is a very important study to consider. As a water and energy being, you can easily be influenced by the vibrational messages floating around you from the collective consciousness 24/7. Your child is receiving those same messages day in and day out, potentially getting programmed, unless you, her coach and leader, show her another way. It's a lot to manage. Don't let it overwhelm you. I'll show you and your child how to hold your own energetic bubbles so that you can be in this world but not be of the world.

First, it starts with programming the energy field of where you live. Your home is the container for your family, a safe haven from the outside world. Energetically, it is important to program the space with intention. Here are some simple feng shui principles to help you create an energy of empowerment in your home. From the moment you wake up, be sure the images, pictures, furniture, and words your family absorbs through the senses contain only messages of love, beauty, and empowerment. Purge excess clutter and negativity as it will only magnetize more of its kind. Invite gratitude and joy so more will flow with ease. Greet each other with a smile of the heart and an embrace with uplifting words. Based on what you do, they will follow in like-kind.

You can create a culture and routine that is in alignment with your family values. If your family was a team of like-minded souls who chose to come here together to fulfill a mission or adventure (which you are), what kind of values would support and guide your experience? Take the time to co-create a list of words and find objects, images, and things to fill your home with that is in alignment with your values. We created a painting of our value words and hung it in our dining room as a constant reminder. It pulls everyone together and leads us toward a shared vision and life goal. By putting an emphasis on your environment, you are programming everyone's subconscious mind every day. Our family enjoys a house full of hand drawn family portraits on every door created by our daughter. My bathroom mirror has updated affirmations and stick figure drawings so all who enter will remember to be their true selves. We have family anthems of songs we love. Our two-year-old loves initiating the ritual of family hands-in where we all put our hands on top of each other like a sports team. Our five-year-old loves bringing everyone together into a family hug. We have created a family culture and vibration of love and empowerment. This is programmed into their cells and they can walk confidently in the world knowing that they are loved, protected, and supported. What's even more important than that is teaching them to remain connected to their own Source guidance and intuition within. This serves as their true Source of power. They need us when they are little, but one day they will be set free to run into the world as conscious leaders. As you teach her the energy practices that follow, it will plant the seeds of light to empower her through life.

The next part of programming your home is also very important. When you learn to do this, close your eyes and use your imagination coupled with the power of intention to make it so. Everything is energy and vibration, including your thoughts. With your eyes closed, envision your home as a large bowl with a lid. Imagine a large grounding cord the size of the property going straight down into the center of the Earth. This looks like a huge hollow tube that encompasses the base of your property and home. This tube goes into the Earth. Let all the energies that don't serve the family flush right down to be recycled for the highest good. From your heart space, project pure love, light, and gratitude onto the whole interior of the bowl. Imagine you are standing inside the container and spreading that high vibrational energy onto the insides of all the walls, then the floor and the ceiling. Write the words in large bright letters on all the surfaces. Then, from high above, pull in through the roof the golden white light of Source energy to fill up the entire container. Voila! There you have a home that is programmed physically and energetically to hold a vibrational force field of love and protection.

When the physical environment is in order and the energetic container is vibrationally programmed, you've got a great foundation to support your family's mission in life. Next, you'll put a protective force field around yourself and all willing family members until they learn to do it themselves. This is a daily practice in psychic hygiene. If you would brush your teeth each morning to wash away the germs, this is exactly the same idea. Keeping the integrity of the bubble strong supports your ability to be your full self. Rather than unconsciously pick up other people's expectations, programs, and energetic hooks, you can exercise heightened awareness by cleansing off other people's energies and refreshing the boundary of where your energy ends and another person's begins. Once you strengthen this practice, it will be very obvious when you've slacked on it. If you do, just put your practice in place immediately. Eventually, it will be second nature and immediate where you can put on your force field as quickly and simply as pushing a button.

Imagine this force field as a giant egg-shaped bubble at least three feet all the way around your body. In my mind, I see Leonardo da Vinci's drawing of The Vitruvian Man, where the arms and legs are extended connecting to create a bubble around the body. See yourself standing in the middle of the bubble and make it pink. This is the color of love, which is of a very high vibration. When people interact with you, they will still feel connected to you, rather than cut off and disconnected. Another added benefit, this bubble only allows love energy to penetrate into your space. This is one tool that teaches you how to be in the world but not be affected by the world.

To demonstrate this practice to your child, you can do the following bubble exercise with her. Ask her to follow along with you:

1. Dip your gigantic imaginary bubble wands into the pretend pink bubble mix.

2. Lift the wands and take three big exhales into the wand. Each time you blow, the bubbles get bigger and bigger until at the end, it envelopes each of your entire bodies. With each breath, show with your hands how much bigger the bubble is growing.

3. Now you're each in the middle of your own giant pink bubbles.

4. Explain that her energy is inside her bubble. Outside the bubble is energy from other people and other things. This bubble can keep you safe from outside energies that don't feel good.

Anytime there is a negative situation or moody person around, remind yourself and others to put on their bubble and fill it with Source light. It is healing, cleansing, and protective. A quick version of the bubble exercise is to take the wand and draw a large circle around your body imagining where the bubble goes. The reason this is a daily exercise is because without conscious attention, its power will begin to slip away. Where attention goes, energy flows. Use it at will and as necessary. Feel into it. Spend time being with the energy and experiencing it. Lean into the edge of your energetic boundary. Does it have a temperature, texture, density, tingling sensation, color, or something else you can sense? If not at first, keep at it. By asking yourself to describe and feel into it, you eventually will. Although the energy is subtle at first, the more you do it, the more palpable it becomes. Extend this explorative conversation with your child. She is naturally in tune and you might end up learning from her, too. I know I did! Be curious, ask questions about what she noticed, and let her do the talking. After awhile, she will begin to take the lead and you will step back to listen and follow. Have fun!! In your daily life, be aware of when you can make reference to the bubble or energy. For instance, if you're at the market and someone on the cashier line is obviously super grumpy and out of alignment, immediately put on your bubble. Remind your child to do the same. Later, ask her if she noticed that there was a grumpy energy nearby and whether the bubble helped. It's OK if she didn't notice. By regularly pointing out these types of instances, you can help her begin to pay attention.

Many times, people on the path of enlightenment begin to get lighter energetically. Grounding into the Earth is an exercise that will serve you well. It is supportive, healing, nurturing, and nourishing. It will allow you to send all the challenging emotions and feelings straight into the Earth to be recycled for the highest good. The description below is simplified for children.

Grounding Exercise:

1. Have everyone on their feet. This is even better if you can do it outside on a patch of grass, sand, or ground. Otherwise, it is still excellent to practice from anywhere.

2. Imagine tree roots growing from the bottoms of your feet all the way down into the ground. To demonstrate, you can draw a picture or show what roots look like.

3. Ever so gently bounce your body up and down to shake the energy loose so the yucky parts come off.

4. Take a deep breath.

5. When you let it out, imagine using the power of your breath to push all the yuckies down through your roots and into the Earth. You can give the downward pushing breath a power sound like "*Sshooo.*" Repeat as necessary.

6. Raise your arms like tree branches and feel relaxed as you gently sway from side to side.

7. Arms down. Smile. Feel how good clearing your space is.

A modified version is to put a hula-hoop on the ground and have your child stand in the middle. Ask her to imagine sending the hoop, like a big hollow tube, all the way down into the center of the earth. Drawing pictures is also helpful to enhance the imagery. Repeat Steps 3 to 7.

Now that the protective bubble is on and the roots are in place to flush out impurities, the next move is to call in Source energy to fill up the bubble. It is the life force that is present in everything everywhere. This creative Source energy is healing, loving, and empowering. It is intelligent, protective, and wise.

Connecting to Source:

1. Raise your arms to the sky and have your child imagine pulling the warm golden sun energy of Source through the top of her bubble. Pull your arms down and touch the top of your bubble show-ing her the energetic path.

Take a moment to enjoy the warmth and love as it envelopes you. Ask her if she feels anything. If she does, help her find new words to describe what she senses. Keep it light and fun.

In addition to Source energy, there is a realm of unseen helpers, including guides, angels, archangels, masters, teach-ers, loved ones, fairies, elementals, and more. These entities are eager to help at a moment's notice. Due to each person's free will and choice as a human, however, they can't inter-vene unless you specifically call on them. They wish more people would call on them for support, so exposing this set of helpers to your child early on would be extremely pow-erful. You're gifting her with a personal spiritual posse of helpers and guides. Depending on your intention and needs of the day, your request will change often. The key here is to build a relationship with them, as you would with a good friend. Don't wait until there is an issue to call on them. Commune with them often so you can further develop your abilities to sense their presence, support, and love. They are here for you. Rather than having a set of steps to teach your child about calling in angels, it's more about making them real and talking about them.

Calling in the Unseen Helpers:

1. Plant a fairy garden and discuss how some people can see fairies and elementals. Doreen Virtue has many books on this topic.

2. Find beautiful pictures of angels and teach her that these helpers are always around her waiting to keep her safe, loved, and happy. Let her know that all she has to do is call on them. Hang a picture of one she chooses or buy a little one for her room. Give her some phrases to start her off with, like *"Angels, I feel scared. Please come now."* Then, ask if she felt a shift or presence. Ask what she felt and just listen. Having an adult to expose her to these subjects and further, to have a parent who is interested in her personal experience in this realm is very affirming. It validates her abilities and opens the way for her to develop even further.

3. Talk about your own experience with your guides, angels, and helpers. This introduces the dialogue as a normal subject.

4. Before bed, you can call in four angels to stand
   at the four corners of the bed facing outward with
   wings outstretched and interlaced. See them glowing with the gossamer fluorescence all through the
   night so she may sleep with prayerful dreams. You
   can say it aloud and ask her to feel the dome of
   angel energy encapsulating her and the bed. You
   can extend this out to stand at the four corners of
   your home or property, too.

Physically, there are some tools that are excellent for regulat-
ing energy. These hyper-sensitive children are often empathic
and able to absorb other people's energy from the world. They
are healers filtering out the negative energy through their
bodies and processing them for the good of the planet. They
need practical tools to support their mission or they will not
last and will have a very challenging life. Whether they are
having an enormous or mild emotional breakdown, the emotional freedom technique (EFT) or tapping as it is known, is
helpful to many. It utilizes the same philosophies as, Tradi-
tional Chinese Medicine, TCM to keep energy flowing and
relieve emotional dis-ease. Tapping specific energy points on
the meridian promotes free flow of energy, hence moving the
stuck emotions out. You can visit www.MaryTanEmpowers.
com and sign up to watch our free videos on how to tap. As her
coach, do it with her, teach her, and have fun with it.

Crystals are created under different conditions with varying combinations of elements making them all special in their
own unique way. Following is a list of empowering crystals
that are excellent for grounding, protecting, and calming the

body. You can place them in your home according to your taste or create a crystal grid to blanket your entire home with the energy signature of the stones you choose. Experiment with placing them under your child's bed or in her room. If it is too energetic and energizing her when it's time to sleep, then place them on a bookshelf nearby instead. Usually, the larger the piece, the stronger its impact. The simplest way to grid is to place large pieces of crystals on the four corners of your land, home, apartment, or bedroom. After cleansing them in salt water or letting them sit in the sunshine for a day, it is clear of past programs, as most do pick up energies. Once it is cleansed, come to a centered place of clarity and intention in your heart. Send your energy of love and protection into the stone intending that each piece will hold that vibration for the highest good. Stay in a meditative state until all pieces are in place. Give thanks and know that all is well. You can have a collection in your child's room for personal use. You can make or buy necklaces, rings, and bracelets that your child can wear.

Here is a short, yet powerful, list:

- Grounding: Shungite, shungite elite, hematite, pyrite, smoky quartz
- Protection: Black tourmaline, smoky quartz, amethyst, black obsidian, and any black stone
- Calming: Blue calcite, blue lace agate, lepidolite, clear quartz, rose quartz

Take her to a crystal shop. Let her explore by walking around carefully and ask her to use her intuition to feel which pieces are calling her attention. When she senses an energetic pull, she can gently hold the piece with you by her side, facilitating the process. Let her examine and feel the energy, then ask her how it feels and if she likes it. As she has the freedom to explore and discover the experience between her body and these crystals, she will find the ones she absolutely must have. It will be interesting to see what she picks. Then go on Google to look up the spiritual qualities.

Essential oils are also incredible in managing moods and health. It takes a tremendous quantity of a single type of flower or herb to create a bottle of high quality oil. Be sure to look for oils that are pure and of the best quality, especially if you are ingesting or applying it on your body. Here is a list of oils to ward off negative energies and calm the body system:

Lavender, Rose, Frankincense, Myrrh, Cypress, Juniper, Sage, Cedarwood, YlangYlang, Clary Sage, Bergamot, Basil, Marjoram, Peppermint, Palo Santo.

In the 1930s England, Edward Bach dedicated his life to researching the healing qualities of plant life and created a line of products capturing the benefits of flower essences. They contain the vibrational signature of the flowers and herbs and when taken under the tongue, the oils enter the body rapidly to offer healing qualities. While the solution is a tincture, it typically includes a mix of brandy to extract the flower essences. There is a child formula, however, that is alcohol free. You can find it under the name of *Rescue Remedy for Kids*. With all the information offered here and in this book, the most important thing for you and your child is always to use your intuition. A coach knows that there's no "one size fits all" approach and solution to anything. So when you're with your child, present the tools in times of need in a way where she has the option to choose which ones will suit her best in that moment. Every moment requires something different.

Here are some additional tools you can use to empower your child. These tools are an excellent way to help you and your child feel grounded, balanced, and more at ease in the world: earthing, spending time in nature, forest bathing, being at the ocean, finding a quiet space, taking salt baths, listening to sound bowl healing, doing *qi gong*, drumming and dancing it out.

Game to Feel Energy

Here's a fun way to demonstrate what energy feels like. Kids love this. The more you feel energy, the more you will develop the ability to differentiate its qualities. Allowing your child to experience this early on in life will support her in her journey as an empowered conscious leader. Here's how it goes:

1. Come to standing, facing a partner.

2. Each person holds both hands up. Without touching, have the palms facing your partner's palms. Leave about one inch apart.

3. Stay there until you really feel the energy sensation between the two of you.

4. Once the connection is established, each person takes a step backward with hands still facing your partner's hands. Remain there and feel the energetic connection. Have everyone chime in with whether they feel it.

5. Once established, step back. Repeat as many times as you can where you still feel the connection. You'll be surprised to see how far apart your bodies are from one another.

6. Talk about what the energy feels like and offer ideas of descriptive words to expand her vocabulary.

While writing this book, I paused to take a phone interview. While I was on the phone, I started to feel increasingly uncomfortable. My chest started to tighten up and my mood shifted from joyous to anxious. I attempted to coach myself to stay present and hold space for a conversation guided by unconditional love. No matter what I did, I couldn't get into the flow with this person and was relieved to rush off the phone. Wow! What was that about? I mean, it left me feeling intensely agitated and overrun with an energy of nervousness. I felt pain in my chest. My mind was searching for meaning and I started to make up stories. But as I used my discernment to feel into them, none of them made sense – none of them felt *right*.

I returned to work at my laptop and then it suddenly hit me like a ton of bricks. As an empath myself, I can feel other people's feelings. I am vigilant with my spiritual practices to protect myself, and yet energies still slip through at times. Because I'm persistent in my practices, it can catch me off guard, especially if I think I've already put my force field on. This is a perfect example that having self-awareness is a total lifesaver. Rather than continue my day feeling anxious, nervous, tight in my chest, ungrounded, fearful, and full of pain in my heart, I fortunately had the awareness to realize what was really going on. It occurred to me that I had absorbed this lady's energy during our phone call. Her insecurities were bubbling over in her mind and affecting the emotional and vibrational layers of her body. As she existed in that state, her vibration emanated out of her, like a powerful epicenter. If unaddressed, over time this energy could get trapped inside a room she spends a significant amount of time in, like in her home. Then, it can become a negative cycle where she re-absorbs the energy, feels the same negativity and slides into a downward spiral. If the energy gets trapped in a space, then there are *feng shui* and energy practices you can use to clear it. As soon as I realized what was going on, I quickly used my hands to intentionally pull out all the negative energy from my chest to throw it straight into an imagined tall blue alchemical flame I had put up in the corner of the room. It is a magical flame that neutralizes all negativity into nothing. I continued pulling the substance out from my chest until I could breathe and recalibrate to love again. The reality is that many people live their lives with these harmful energies circulating in and around their bodies without the tools to empower their personal state of being. The person on the phone didn't intentionally send me her negative energies that were created from her stormy thoughts of insecurity. She simply didn't have the training to transform her state and it spilled out into everything she did. Sound is vibrational – her words, her thoughts, her feelings, her intentions – and they are capable of being transferred instantly regardless of space and time. Rather than allow the domino effect to pass like a virus from person to person, anyone with the knowledge can change the pattern on the spot. You can do exactly what I did above.

Train yourself by practicing it every day and over time, you will become masterful. This is something you can do for your child while she's in an emotional breakdown. You can pull out the negative energies from the top of her head, center of her heart or anywhere from her space and throw it into the fire. Then, envelope her in white light and love. Here are the steps you can practice yourself:

1. Self-Awareness: catch yourself when you are feeling a negative emotion. Identify where in your body the sensation is occurring. Is it a knot in your stomach, tight chest, achy shoulders, headache, anxiety, anger, or moodiness? When teaching your child, you can broadcast what you are doing to yourself in real time. If she is having a tough day, invite her to come to you when she's ready to feel better because you can help her. When she comes, do the process to her as you explain each step along the way.

2. Fire Alchemy: imagine a tall blue flame in the corner of the room. Your imagination and intention will make it so. Children are very in tune with their imagination so this will be easy.

3. Extract Negativity: use your hands and pull the negative emotion or sensation out and throw it straight into the alchemical fire. Repeat as needed until you are fully relieved. When you throw the negativity into the fire, tune into the substance as if it were tangible. Throw it as if it had weight and

even give it a sound effect as it flies across the room. This makes it more real to your child.

4. Fill with Love: breathe in love and fill in all the spaces that have been cleared out. Again, give this energy a color, texture, weight, temperature, or sound. Make it real for her. It will feel so good as it circulates within and around the body. Take your time soaking it in.

5. Protection: make sure you have your bubble on and strengthen the outer layer. Simply tune into your feeling senses to see if it is there and ensure that it is fortified. This happens through your intention and imagination as well.

This is definitely a practice you can teach your child. As you coach her through the learning process, she is gaining the muscle memory to: 1) Be self-aware; 2) Take responsibility for her own state of being; 3) Know how to take the steps to change her state to an empowering one; and finally, as a natural consequence, 4) be a leader of herself and to those around her. Rather than be passively led by others, she can powerfully lead.

Here's an incredible example that shocked me. One day, I was going through my own emotional growth spurt (that's what I call it. We are growing all the time and sometimes it can be emotional and challenging). So, there I was, having a hard time processing "my stuff" and what was heartwarming was watching my five-year-old do all the things I usually do for her. First, she evaluated the situation. That's Step

1. She asked if maybe I was hungry and experiencing low blood sugar. So, she instantly ran off and returned with water and trail mix. That didn't seem to work so she continued to analyze the scenario. She followed Step 2 of the EMPOWER Method and made herself fully available to me. She put down all her toys and activities. She turned off any source of possible distractions. Then, she really blew me away! She started to implement Step 3 by putting on her coaching hat. She was curious about what the cause of my discomfort was. She tuned in energetically and began to pull out the negative energy from the top of my head and threw it into an alchemical fire she had erected in the corner of the room. I didn't catch onto all that she was doing until I felt a dramatic shift in my state only to notice her standing behind me pulling out all my yucky energies. It is moments like these when you know that all the hard work you have invested in has paid off. I was beyond impressed and grateful for this precious empathic child to do great work in the world. Put these tools into practice for yourself and teach them to your child. You too will have these moments of awe in your life.

You, amazing woman, came into this world to lead. Your child came into this world to grab the baton from you and run into the world lighting the way for all who seek it. One of the invisible armors to wear is the protective force field that keeps out the negative energies and programs dominating the ethers today. When enough individuals wake up to the leader within and ripple out the power of consciousness, the tide will change to a world thriving with love. The one who practices putting on her protective field each morning is like the one who has worn her life vest capable of helping others to shore. That is you. More importantly, that makes you available to coach your child to do the same.

CHAPTER 7

Step 4:
Offer a Safe Space

*"The key to growth is the introduction
of higher dimensions of consciousness
into our awareness."*

–Lao Tzu

S o, your child is in the middle of a breakdown or putting up a fight. It's intense. What next? Here's Step 4. Offer her a safe space defined by unconditional love, heightened curiosity, deep listening, and one that is devoid of personal agenda, other than love. How do you do that when it's been a long day for you and this is the last thing you want to deal with? You're a wife and a mom and you're exhausted. You crave a good night's sleep and a bubble bath with a glass of bubbly. Well, as they say, the days are long and the years are short. It is exactly in these times when you shall remind yourself who you really are – a soul in human form here to coach your child with the tools of light. Part of the process includes providing the safe space for her to discover herself in this world. The external environment is constantly imposing its expectations and scripts onto the people. Its overarching vibratory frequency oscillates around fear, lack, and stories of what the symbols of success look like. The antidote is to consistently exercise personal transformation to transcend the symptoms of stress, suppressed emotions, and undigested traumas as a way to reveal authentic wholeness. Write your own stories of Source-guided success exemplified by love, abundance, and bliss.

You are a powerful spirit who chose to come to Earth at this specific time with a purpose and a mission. In order to come into a physical world, you had to materialize from an etheric ephemeral nature into a dense physical being. In this world, ruled by duality, there is hot and cold, white and black, up and down. There's a lot of energy swirling about out there in the world. Some light, some dark, some conscious, some unconscious. Some energies have an agenda and others don't. The duality can seem confusing to a child and even make her feel unsafe in this big scary world. These are all two sides of the same coin. In this dimension, you cannot have one without the other. It doesn't mean you are helpless and must passively receive whatever is dealt you. Certainly, you could choose that route, but how enjoyable is that? Not very. To be immune to victimhood, you must claim your queenhood and recognize who you really are. Climb that mountain and mount your throne so you may rule with perspective, clarity, and Source-guided power.

As a queen, you will put on a regal crown that represents your devotion to mental mastery. It starts with taking responsibility for your thoughts, feelings, and actions. This is your ability to respond rather than react to emotional triggers. The next step is to practice vigilant self-awareness. This is when you are able to step outside of your perspective and witness yourself from a higher stance. Meditation is the cornerstone of strengthening this ability. When you meditate, you are clearing the communication line between you and your higher self. Why step into your role as a queen? When you're empowered, you're more able to create that safe space and show your child the way.

Your physical body is but a small fraction of your whole energetic existence. This body is an expression, extension, and projection of Source energy. It's as if you are playing a video game, like Street Fighter. You, the one holding this book right now, are the character on the screen. So, who's directing all your moves? The one holding the remote control is your higher self. That higher self has an enormously wider perspective even beyond the storyline on the screen. There are other things happening in the next room and out across the world. If you are distracted and pulled in by the excitement of the daily drama, the broader perspective of life gets lost. Opportunities go unnoticed; the things you pray for pass by unrecognized. Zoom out. Be like the hawk on the tree and stop, looking into the horizon noticing every little movement below. This is expanded awareness. This is how you can rule one step removed from emotions and exercise crystal clear equanimity. The clarity and non-attachment makes it possible to show up as the grounded and balanced self who is able to nurture a space of unconditional love.

If your higher self is the one holding the remote control, does that mean you're off the hook? Does that mean you can go back to sleep and just let it make all the moves? To live a powerful life of purpose and intentional creations, you will need to partner with your higher self. When you do the spiritual work to clear the illusions from the mind, you will reach a point where you actually want your higher self to take over the steering wheel of life, as a partner. You begin to acknowledge and understand that you co-create your reality with this other aspect of yourself. You, the character on the screen, are the one experiencing the *reality* on screen. The higher self would not have the opportunity to taste this cornucopia of experiences if it weren't for your physical existence. While you are here in a body having emotions, ideas, and experiences, you are sending requests for more of this and less of that. It's kind of like if the character could send messages saying, "Move me left, move me right." When the character realizes its role in relation to the higher self, it could send the information up, then relax knowing that the higher self will make the appropriate moves and adjustments, as requested. No, you are not off the hook in life. You cannot go back to sleep now that you've expanded consciously. You can't ask a butterfly to squeeze back into the body of a caterpillar. You have become that butterfly by expanding your mind. The beauty is, you get to co-create your reality by sending the messages up to your higher self, knowing that this request or something better will present itself in divine right time. It's exciting to regain pieces of your innate power as you become an active participant in the game of your life. The more you reclaim, the more fun you will have.

After putting on the crown to protect your mind of negative programs, thoughts, and energies, you'll put on a thick velvet cape. This cape of protection represents your dedication to taking care of your physical body. It also includes engaging in a daily practice to maintain the integrity of your energetic force field. Then, imagine holding a scepter in your hand. This scepter represents your ability to connect heaven and earth through your physical self. This is the junction between spirit and body as you create in this world. It is where the higher self and human form, the heart and mind, meet to manifest for the highest good of all. From this vantage point, you can lead your troops into the field spreading the net of light across the globe. When you awaken and refine yourself to claim your queendom, then your tribe of sisters will flock to your light and leadership. It is in that moment where you've lit the light in their hearts to lead themselves, their families, and children to higher ground. It is then that the light revolution explodes with such magnificence that observers of all dimensions will benefit from the ripple effect. It all begins with you carving a new path, which creates the safe space for others to follow suit.

As a human here on Earth, you must realize that this is all like a game. Like a child in school, we are experiencing play-based learning. The part of you that never dies is this energetic, spiritual soul aspect of you. Your body will eventually disintegrate, and then you get to write a whole new adventure of a lifetime to play out again in the next incarnation. It'll be filled with twists and turns, dramas and challenges, joys and happiness. On the higher planes, duality no longer exists. The physical aspect goes away, time and space do not exist and everything is out in the open. There are no more secrets nor a need to hide as every being is connected, united, and aware. Love is the tonality of this existence. For a being of that dimension, can you see that coming into a world of duality is like a game? It's the same reason people are glued to the screen when watching drama-filled movies. You're experiencing all these heightened emotions vicariously in the safety of your own seat.

Because you chose to come to the dense plane of Earth school, let's take a closer look at this body you live in. There is a limiting belief in the collective consciousness that humans can live to about 100 years old. It claims that as the body ages, it must suffer disease and pain. This however is not true at all! In 2017, the oldest verified person to die in modern times did so at 146 years old. There are reports of Chinese herbalists and martial artists who died in recent times at 250 and 500 years old. The beliefs in the collective consciousness are there because the majority of the world population agrees to it. When we shift the amount of people who hold a certain belief, then larger paradigm shifts occur. If you are not intentionally programming your own beliefs in your mind and cells, then you are leaving yourself wide open to act out this lifetime ruled by what the mass consciousness believes. Be aware, this is not for you. When you cultivate the lifestyle of questioning everything you've ever known and using your intuition and discernment to feel into what is true, then you are in your power position – awake and aware.

Extend this level of conscious thinking to your daily life with your family and child. Teaching your child to trust her own intuition and discernment will give her a huge leg up in navigating through this often confusing world. Showing her that it's OK not to agree just to be liked, loved, or to fit in gives her permission early on to trust herself and her inner presence. As she develops this important relationship within herself, she will gain the qualities of confidence, strength, and security in this world. None of those can be taken away from her unless she forgets this connection and gives away her power. How do you have such conversations? When she asks whether she should do this or that, put the decision back in her court. This will teach her how to create her own level of safety in this world. Ask her to feel into it. Does one choice feel more open or constricting in the heart? Or does one feel more warm and fuzzy or tight and uncomfortable in the gut? If at first she does not know, that's OK. By posing the question, she will begin to tune into the possibility of knowing next time. You are essentially opening up the conversation and thought process for her to find out on her own. This is how she will learn to create a safe space for herself. If she can answer these questions, then you can explain what they mean. The open and nurturing feeling is a positive sign that is in alignment with her highest good. The constriction and discomfort is a sign that it is not nurturing nor would it serve her highest good. Giving her the awareness to tune in and a language to talk about it paves the way for increased awareness.

Since we live in this vehicle of a body, it would be empowering to find out how to take care of it. Imagine riding in a speeding car that does not have doors or seatbelts. Would you feel scared? Of course you would. If this body was sick and missing the equivalent of all its doors and seatbelts, it would feel scary to be alive, too. Therefore, teaching her how to have a healthy body and how to understand the messages of her body wisdom is a huge way to fortify that sense of security.

As we examine this body and how to utilize it optimally, here are some inspirational people alive today who have redefined what is possible for the human body. Ernestine Shepherd is an 80-year-old bodybuilding competitor who wakes up at 2:30 a.m. to train her body. She didn't start going to the gym until she was 56 and she started competing at 71. This led to her winning many trophies. Annette Larkins is a 73-year-old raw vegan practicing woman who appears decades younger. Without surgery or artificial means, she appears to look like she is in her 40s, maintaining an abundant level of vibrancy and vivaciousness. A woman named Jasmuheen has practiced breatharianism for more than 25 years and travels the world teaching people about this ancient regimen found in India and China. Breatharians do not require food and water for sustenance. They live off of life force energy known as *prana* and do a specialized practice that is not for everyone. There is a set of parents in California who have been practicing this for nearly a decade. All of these examples are to show that what the masses believe is not necessarily true. If one person can do it, then the possibility exists for all. Begin to open your thinking and question everything you were taught. Use your own discernment and ability to feel into whether something is true of the highest sense. Once you begin to peel back the layers, more light will flood into your reality. This is where it gets exciting. The more inner work you do, the more light you can hold. The more you can hold, the more light you attract and receive. The more light you receive, the more you exude and the ripple effect radiates out in cascading waves.

While you're here, you might as well have a comfortable ride in this vehicle. Not only is it your ride, it is also the sacred temple for your soul. As of 2017, the number one cause of death globally for the last 15 years is heart disease. Why is your heart, the seat of consciousness, life, and love, most susceptible to injury and death? How can we shore up its safety? We all know that getting ample exercise, eating a healthy diet, and managing stress are important to heart health, but what else is at play here? In TCM, the heart is considered the king of all organs. It rules all the organs in the body and those organs will sacrifice their energy to support the health of the heart. What causes the heart to lose harmony? In TCM, the heart is the source of all thoughts, ideas, mental focus, planning, intelligence, and thought processes. Overthinking, or churning concerns over and over again in your mind, can negatively impact the heart's energy. Whether you're a high-level executive constantly working at elevated levels of stress at a job you despise, or you're a parent who carries the self-imposed weight of the world with guilt, these are all mental actions burning off the heart's energy. These are all unnecessary ways of showing up in the world. Why would someone work themselves to death or over give until she falls ill? It all goes back to the unconscious beliefs and scripts people buy into from their upbringing through family stories, cultural programming, the media, and other influences. People are being bombarded by messages all the time. Someone who isn't aware that watching the news and drama filled shows are actually programming their thoughts, feelings, and life experiences, might spend much of their time in a low vibrational state of fear and worry. This same person who is unconsciously being programmed by the collective beliefs with lack and anger isn't open to the tools of transformation yet, because they haven't questioned what else is possible. Question everything. The emotion associated with the heart is joy. When thoughts circle around without end, depleting the energy of the heart, then the joy begins to dissipate with it. How many corporate executives have we heard of who overwork themselves, lose the joys of life while taking on more stresses and suddenly drop dead at their desk, all in the name of success? This heart of yours contains the spark of consciousness. It is the meeting point between heaven, Earth, and human. As the queen, you must rule with equanimity from this meeting place. Your scepter represents the ability to receive Source guidance while in human form and manifest it out into the world with the vibrating consciousness of light. This is the gift of empowerment to endow your child with. Don't allow the system and intentional misprogramming of the world to dictate a misguided script of success that leads to an unfulfilled life of stress and dissipating joy. Rather, empower her with the gifts of consciousness, intuition, discernment, energy management, emotional intelligence, and a personal connection to Source. Show her how to climb the mountain to mount her throne. Show her what it means to wield the power of the crown, cape, and scepter.

Part of taking care of this amazing vehicle is stress management. Not only does it keep us healthier, but also it allows us to create an emotionally safer space for our child. Instead of focusing on the stressful thoughts of the past or future, we can return to the present and offer a peaceful energy rather than the disruptive ones of fear and worry. For the last 26 years, the HeartMath Institute has dedicated itself to researching and spreading the tools of heart health. If stress leads to hypertension – a huge factor in heart disease – then reducing stress is a solution to lowering the rate of heart disease. Stanford University utilized the HeartMath program in a study and found significant improvements in patients with congestive heart failure. They were able to reduce stress and depression by incorporating a three-step method called the Quick Coherence Technique, a scientifically based tool to bridge the heart-mind connection. The steps are as follows: 1) Focus on slow breathing on the heart; 2) Think about something you can be grateful for or something that makes you feel good. This is simple enough that even a child can do it. You could show her how to put one hand on top of another and rest it on her heart space. Then invite her to breathe slowly and deeply into this place. Within one breath, everyone will be saying "Ahh, that feels so good. That's what a safe space feels like." This practice echoes the teachings of Abraham-Hicks' the Law of Attraction. One of the elements in the equation of attracting what you desire is to think the *next better thinking thought*, especially when you are vibrating low. The reason for this is because, as vibrational beings living in a vibrational world, we attract the beliefs we most think about consciously and subconsciously. In this way, to think about something you can be grateful for or something that makes you feel good will lead you up the vibrational staircase to a place where you will attract more things to feel good about. When you feel good, stress goes down, blood pressure decreases, and the heart can re-establish homeostasis.

The more tools we can teach our children to manage and transform stress and disappointment, the better. Research shows that people who hold onto anger, resentment, and blame suffer more health problems. HeartMath founder Doc Lew Childre, Jr. states that *forgiving and releasing old hurts from your system is like taking a mental and emotional bath.* It is imperative to clean out this buildup of toxic emotions, just as you would clear out clogged pipes in your house. There is an ancient Hawaiian practice of reconciliation and forgiveness called Ho'oponopono. The word itself means "to make right." This extends to making right with yourself, the people you are having a challenge with, and with your ancestors. Based on four simple steps, the technique's effects are profound and life altering. You can do this in person with someone or you can invite their energetic higher self to come sit in front of you. When working with your ancestors, it would be the same process. When working with yourself, you can call in a part of yourself you've been judging or unhappy with. Once you are with the person or energetic representation of the one you are seeking to make right with, these are the four steps to follow. Take your time in each stage and really experience the moment.

1. I'm sorry. Express whatever you feel sorry about. It could be you owning some part of the discord or feeling sorry for the situation in general. It could be feeling sorry that things turned out the way

it did. As long as you are earnest and authentic, that's the most important part of this step.

2. Please forgive me. Ask for them to hear you and forgive you or the situation.

3. Thank you. Say thank you and feel gratitude for a reconciliation. It's freeing when everyone can let it go. That is truly something to be thankful for.

4. I love you. Show love by saying it out loud, "I love you."

Imagine you two shaking hands, hugging, or having a sign of completion. When you can forgive and feel forgiven, you have reclaimed the energy leakage that happens when people harbor and suppress negative feelings. It takes so much energy to hold down unprocessed emotions. This is a way to transform that and take one step closer to wholeness and freedom.

When I have shown up in a way that isn't in alignment with my highest and best self, I own it as soon as possible. For example, one morning, I was feeling stressed with so many things piling up on my To Do list, I inadvertently took it out on my five-year-old daughter. I was snappy and cranky. When I was able to catch myself, I immediately came down to my child's eye level and used this forgiveness process to regain a safe space for her. It served our relationship on so many levels. First, it showed that I am not perfect and that I am willingly working on it by taking responsibility for myself. I didn't judge or shame myself. I simply owned it and took positive action to rectify it. The bonus to this is she will learn that she doesn't have to be perfect either. She will learn to value self-awareness and the persistence to always get back up and try again. Second, it demonstrates healthy communication and how to use the process. Lastly, the four steps allow us to authentically resolve the discord energetically and emotionally so no one feels the need to harbor negative feelings of being hurt or feeling guilty. It instantly transforms the situation and the people involved. We were both free to return to the safe space of love.

It has been shown that the heart's magnetic field radiates outside the body and can affect others. Whether you are in the midst of witnessing your child's emotional breakdown or a challenge with your coworker, you have the intangible power to affect the situation. First, slow down your breathing. Next, imagine breathing universal unconditional love in through your soul into your heart space. Then, slowly exhale that unconditional love from your heart and out into the situation or the person's space. Continue this until you begin to feel a shift. It is subtle. Just as you can't see the wind, you can certainly witness the aftermath of what it can do in a powerful storm. You hold the invisible power of unconditional love and can harness it through intentional thought and breath. The next time you are in the position of coaching your child through a challenging moment, use this intentional form of breathing to attune and adjust the vibratory frequency of her space. She will feel the waves of loving kindness and non-judgmental acceptance emanating from your being. This creates the environment supportive of her transformation.

The human body is amazing! Doing all that you can to keep it healthy and vibrating high will offer an existence of overall wellness and good feelings. Have you ever noticed that when you're nervous, anxious, or stressed, your stomach gets upset? Have you had a gut instinct about a situation that turned out to be spot on? Your gut is called "the second brain" because it uses more than 30 neurotransmitters and creates 95 percent of serotonin, the happy hormone. An imbalance of serotonin levels is linked to heart disease and depression. Knowing how to support this intimate two-way gut-brain communication channel will offer another tool to raise your child's vibrations and consciousness. Your body has so much wisdom seeded within it. Here are a few basic tips to support a healthy gut environment to positively influence your child's emotional state and mood. It's true that we are what we eat. Sometimes feeling out of control in this world can be traced back to eating foods that disrupt the hormones and mood functions of the body. To cross off this cause of feeling unsafe in the world, first, eliminate foods that may be irritating to the body. Some common ones are eggs, wheat, and cheese. You can easily research a long list of possible allergens. If there aren't any food sensitivities or allergies, continue by taking a quality probiotic and prebiotic. These good bacteria will help digest the foods eaten creating a thriving gut environment. Lastly, bone broth and collagen are additional elements used to strengthen the stomach lining and prevent disease, like leaky gut syndrome. There is an entire school of thought in Chinese Medicine that is built on the same belief that optimal health begins in the gut. Eating in a way to elevate your child's physical health will affect her vibration. Elevating her vibration will lift her mood. When she has the tools to positively impact her health, vibration, and mood, she is in the power position to command a safe space no matter where she is.

It's important to recognize the major causes of death because we're examining how to utilize this body vehicle optimally. We're also connecting the dots between the limiting beliefs of the collective consciousness and its manifestations on the health of the people. To be aware is to bring the power back to your ability to live in this world and feel authentically safe. If you're constantly battling physical ailments and disease, your existence will be riddled with fear and worry. Once you are aware, then you can empower your child. You came into this incarnation to fulfill a soul purpose. Without a strong, healthy body, it won't be as enjoyable of a ride. If you're here to serve, why not serve in a comfortable ride?

The second biggest cause of death around the world is lung disease. Physiologically, there are many factors that impact lung health. Depending on where you live, there's outdoor and indoor air pollution, whether or not you smoke, and if the type of work you do exposes you to different conditions. Examining this from another angle, in TCM, emotions are the major internal causes of disease. The lungs are associated with the emotions of grief and anxiety. There is a dominance of unresolved grief in the lives of many across the globe. The common habit of brushing little hurts under the rug rather than bravely communicating the truth accumulates to harm the lung. The world is also largely stressed out with the anxiety to perform, to be someone, to do something all from the perspective of satisfying some internal critic or external expectation. Neither of those are empowering or authentic because it's not connected to the inner presence of the Source energy. It plays only into the egoic and personality mind of wanting to be liked and accepted. It wants to finally prove that it really is good enough and lovable. The confusing life experience of wanting joy but feeling not good enough is due to the incongruence between the conscious and subconscious minds. It is also a symptom of the soul and mind being out of alignment. A lifetime of unprocessed traumas experienced on a global scale is the overwhelming level of undigested grief harming the lungs leading to the second greatest cause of death on the planet. It is imperative that the youth of this world learn how to become conscious beings armed with the tools of personal transformation. There is no need to suppress negative emotions in order to appear happy, put together, or acceptable. When enough people stop plugging into the channels of misinformation and lead themselves with mental and emotional mastery, then change on a grand scale is possible. This type of mastery begins at the level of the thought and is built upon the foundation of meditation. These are tools and life skills to help your child create an authentically safe space of self-acceptance and self love.

The beliefs your mind hold are contributing to the overall signature of the collective consciousness. The collective consciousness holds the beliefs of what the majority of the world population believes. At the same time, the people of the world are programmed by the vibration of what the collective consciousness holds. And there you see the cyclical action. Which came first, the chicken or the egg? It doesn't matter. What matters is that you have the power to end the cycle and lead it in a direction that serves the highest high. You do that by engaging your awareness and exercising your right to use your free will and choice with consciousness. If unprocessed emotions are the greatest internal cause of disease, then teaching your child how to recognize, process, and transform her emotions will lead to a more powerful and successful life experience.

Another factor that affects how your child feels and shows up in the world is completely invisible. Knowledge is power and the more you know, the more you have the opportunity to balance yourselves in other ways. If you don't know, then you end up going about your day feeling out of control emotionally. When a child is in this state, it is an indicator or cause that she is no longer feeling safe in this world. There are subtle planetary factors that impact how we feel, act, and operate as a human. Everything in this dimension has a vibrational signature. Love vibrates at 528 hertz (Hz), that's why listening to 528 Hz music is healing and a great way to attune yourself to a higher vibration. Emotions, thoughts, and objects all have vibrational signatures. Even the Earth has its own signature called the Schumann resonance. For a long period of time, Earth was vibrating at 7.83 Hz, but it has been steadily rising. As of July 2017, it has risen all the way up past 30 Hz. Dr. Kathy Forti, a clinical psychologist, inventor, and author, looked deeper into the fluctuations in search of meaning. Interestingly enough, the Schumann frequency fluctuations relate to the human brain wave and heart rate. The rise in vibratory frequency is elevating the mind from a relaxed alpha/theta state to greater states of mental awakening. Simultaneously, over the last 2,000 years, the magnetic field of the Earth has been weakening, and even more so recently. Dr. Forti recalls an old Indian sage saying, "The magnetic field of Earth was put in place by the Ancient Ones to block out primordial memories...so souls could learn unhampered by memories of our true heritage." The magnetic field changes are loosening those memory blocks, lifting the veil of amnesia. This certainly explains why so many people around the world are suddenly waking up to who they really are and discovering their innate spiritual gifts coming strongly to the fore. Many adults waking up suddenly are wondering what in the world happened to them. They are having to search for answers to make sense of this drastic change. Without a proper guide, the children can have an even harder time adjusting to all of this. Having awareness of this planetary shift offers an added layer of understanding to how our bodies are sensitive and affected by different forces. Taking it one step further, we see that it gives insight into how it is influencing your child's body, mental frequencies, and emotional states. It's affecting everyone, including the children.

The next time you find her in the middle of an emotional breakdown, stop and create the ultimate safe space. Bubble her with a loving energetic force field and contain her energy. Put on your own bubble for the same reasons. Next, place a bubble over the both of you as the sacred space of transformation. Put a grounding cord beneath this larger bubble and let it hook into the center of the Earth. From above, connect Source energy into it to fill the bubble with universal love. Breathe in unconditional love and exhale it into her space. Enter the sacred container slowly and respectfully with her boundaries in mind. This will allow her to feel safe and to not have to receive any expectations and imposed ways of being. She will then have the space to authentically feel, process, and release these new or big emotions. This is you facilitating her learning in the presence of a conscious guide.

There are some amazing practitioners, methodologies, and resources available today that can support you and your child's journey on the path of transformation. Here is a list to start you off, plus some life-affirming concepts. The goal is to experiment with different tools to find the ones that best support the rebalancing of both you and your child's bodies and vibrations. This will, in turn, lift your child's emotions allowing her to feel safe as she is in the world and learn how not to be of the world.

- Chakra Balancing: Chakras are energy centers in the body. The most common seven are found in the midline of the body starting at the base of the spine and rising up to the crown of the head. Regular maintenance in clearing and balancing chakras will help keep the energy flowing through your system to enhance overall health in mind, body, and spirit.

- Meditation: There are numerous ways to meditate. If you're new to it, keep it simple. Find a quiet place, sit comfortably with your back straight, and calm your body to stillness. For adults, spend at least 15 minutes each day breathing deeply and slowly with eyes closed. Leave all expectations at the door and simply enjoy the quietude and sacred connection with your inner self. If we consider prayer a conversation with the divine, then meditation is considered cultivating the ability to listen to divine guidance. For children, spend eight cycles of breath looking at a candle or flower in nature. As tolerance increases, she will know how much time she chooses to spend daily.

- Yoga, Qi Gong, Tai Chi: These are energy practices to cultivate your life force energy in the body. It enhances your health and inner strength. It affects the mind, body, and spirit for a greater connection to Source.

- Crystals: This is an incredible tool to support any goal you have. These intelligent objects hold vibrations that range from cleansing to energizing, protective to empowering. You can use them to grid your home, property, or room for protection from negative energy, electromagnetic radiation, and establish more nurturing vibrations.

- Meridians: These are energy channels in the body affected by acupuncture, herbs, proper food, drink, emotions, and movement. It is a term from TCM.

- Chiropractic Medicine: The spinal cord is like a major cable that exits the brain and travels down inside the spinal column and branches off into spinal nerves to serve the rest of your body. This practice adjusts your spine to relieve pressure and obstruction on your nervous system allowing the free flow of energy, nutrients, and blood.

- Homeopathy: This 200-year-old system is based on the belief that like cures like, meaning a substance taken in small amounts will cure the same symptoms it causes in large amounts. It is free of chemicals and easily found in many health food stores. It can be found in small pellets, pills, tinctures, and other forms.

- Internal Cleanse: There are numerous ways to cleanse your body. You can buy products to target certain organ systems, overall health, or even rid yourself of internal parasites. I love doing a bi-annual green juice cleanse in the spring and fall to gently cleanse and nourish the cells. Keep it gentle and nurturing. Simply shop with an open heart and allow the vegetables and fruits to call to you.

- Clean & Conscious Fuel: Because everything is vibrational, the types of food and drinks you put into your body will contribute to your vibrational health. Making sure that your food is free or reduced of harmful chemicals in pesticides, genetically modified foods, artificial coloring, and preservatives will help lower the overall toxic load humans are exposed to simply by being on Earth at this time. The greater the toxic load, the lower the body vibrates, and therefore the lower the consciousness, mood and life experience. The opposite is also true. Therefore, it is important to lessen the toxic load whenever possible. Every little bit counts because it is cumulative so choose clean water clear of chemicals and fluoride, a chemical linked to Alzheimer's. Fluoride also calcifies the pineal gland, which is the seat of intuition. MSG is a neurotoxin that makes food taste good, but is detrimental to your brain. Look into the long list of common chemicals and their recent renames so you may avoid putting them into your body. Stay up to date on name changes too, because the industry has a habit of trying to make toxins appear less harmful.

- Growth hormones: In America, many companies will use growth hormones and a combination of male and female hormones to yield more milk or meat production at a faster rate. The ultimate goal is to increase the bottom line, but this increase of GH has been linked to developmental, reproductive, and hormonal imbalances as it impacts the pituitary gland, a.k.a. the master gland, which controls many other hormone glands. It is linked to early puberty, a greater risk of breast cancer and obesity. Look into grass-fed and free-range meats at your farmer's market or search online for a reliable delivery service direct from the ranch.

- Cruelty free foods: Avoid ingesting the energetic vibration of fear, sadness, and anger from the way animals are raised and killed before packaging the food for your consumption. Studies show that the increase of adrenaline, the stress hormone, in meats leads more likely to spoilage. That emotional vibration gets passed onto the next being who absorbs it as food. Most mass-produced animal products are raised and slaughtered in a cruel manner causing its meat to be filled with negative emotional vibrations that will later be taken in through a meal. Research where to get conscious goods.

- Fish: Everything is connected in this world. Air pollution from rapidly developing nations like China and India can be measured across the oceans and tracked in countries across the globe. With numerous and recent explosions of nuclear plants pouring radioactive material into our global waters, the sea life, seafood, and sea vegetables are largely contaminated with life-damaging elements once ingested. Farmed fish are often created in waters connected to the global network of the Earth's waterways and not free of the same challenges. At the same time, farmed fish often have injected chemical coloring to appear more beautiful. They are often raised in poor conditions while being fed an unnatural diet due to lower costs. Again, do your research and find sources of conscious foods.

- Pineal Gland: The pineal gland, a.k.a. the third eye, is a pea-sized gland located between the brows and set back in the middle of the head. It is only here that serotonin, the happy hormone, is transformed into melatonin, the sleep regulator.

Science has discovered the same rod-shaped light sensitive cells here, just like the ones found in the retinas of the two outer eyes. It's a place where consciousness is regulated and perception beyond ordinary sight is available. One of the ways to enhance this area is to focus your attention and breathe here during closed eye meditation.

- Reiki: Founded in 1922 by a Japanese Buddhist, Reiki is a way of channeling universal life force energy in through your body and out through your hands onto yourself or others to reduce stress, increase relaxation, and promote the body's own ability to heal. You can find a master teacher to attune you to this energy. At the same time, you can train yourself to call in Source or love energy through the crown of your head and out through your hands for a similar effect.

- Electromagnetic Frequency: Today, it is hard to escape the invisible and constant exposure to electromagnetic field (EMF) radiation emanating from wireless networks, TVs, laptops, cell phones, tablets, cars, and microwaves. Even the International Agency for Research on Cancer (IARC), a component of the World Health Organization, has stated that EMFs are possibly carcinogenic to humans. For that reason, it is worth your time to research ways to protect yourself from this silent yet harmful exposure. I like using the shungite crystal that contains fullerene, a molecular carbon formation that can neutralize many types of EMFs by absorbing and storing these energetic pollutants into its hollow carbon structures. There are many types of products on the market (not all are created equal or effective). Use your intuition and discernment to feel into what is right for you.

- Skin Products: Your skin is the largest organ and absorbs whatever you put on it. The detergent, softener, water, lotion, spray, shampoo, conditioner, sunscreen, makeup, nail polish, and other products you put on it get absorbed into your body. Many of these chemicals have been linked to cancer and reproductive imbalances. Be sure to educate yourself and read the labels to avoid the absorption of harmful chemicals into your body. The American cosmetics industry is largely self-regulated with no requirements from the FDA or federal government for approval before going to market. Consult organizations like the Environmental Working Group (www.EWG.org) for more information.

- Exercise & Weight Training: Moving your body brings oxygen to your cells and improves mood. Weight training, even in small amounts, can strengthen your bone density and lead to a healthier existence. When you're lifting weights, repeat empowering affirmations in your mind with each inhale and exhale. When you push yourself further than you thought you could go, your body expands and so does your mental attitude. Stretching is excellent for letting go of stored stress and emotions. Lean into the stretch as you inhale, then exhale and let it all go. Look into moves to stretch the hips as we store a lot of emotions here, and most people don't think about stretching this part of the body.

- Sleep: In TCM, it is important to go to bed by 10 p.m. This period gives your body the time to rejuvenate each organ. Each organ is associated with a specific time and having enough rest allows it to regenerate and heal.

- Nature: Forest bathing is a common practice in Japan where people go to the forest to spend the day absorbing the healing qualities of the energy and air in that area. Earthing and grounding are also growing in popularity as its life-affirming benefits are documented. By standing barefoot on the Earth, you are able to harmonize the positive and negative ions between your body and the environment. The byproduct of living in modern day Earth are the negative effects it has on the body in the form of food, air, water, pollution, EMFs, and more. Earthing is one way to release and regulate a portion of the harmful charges to re-establish harmony once again.

While there are so many more categories to research, this list is a good start. These are ways to empower your choices to elevate your child's vibration and mood, hence her sense of being OK in the world. Once you begin to scratch the surface, your intuition will naturally guide you to what is most relevant for your highest good. As always, use your own discernment to know what will nurture or deplete you, even the information I share with you. Ultimately, you are the queen in charge of your mind, body, energetic space, and life purpose and mission. Arm yourself with knowledge, wisdom, and daily spiritual practice. The next frontier humanity is embarking on is the spiritual light revolution. In this way, you will be fully capable of walking powerfully into this world while being immune to the agendas heavy in the ethers. You are now awake and aware, hence empowered to choose with consciousness. This is the greatest gift you can give your child. The more areas she can positively influence, the more chances she has of remaining conscious, confident, and connected. The more aspects of her mind, body, spirit, and space that she learns to elevate, the more powerfully she can show up in this world. Hold the vision of a better world close to your heart and ignite it into reality with the fire of your soul. With you as her guide showing her the tools of how to manage her internal and external states, she will be empowered to go out into the world carrying an authentic sense of safety wherever she goes.

CHAPTER 8

Step 5:
Wait for the First Move

*"Nothing ever goes away until it
teaches us what we need to know."*
–Pema Chodron

L et's revisit the scene. She's freaking out over something seemingly miniscule and completely loses all self-composure. Maybe you've repeated yourself for the ump-teenth time and she's still putting up a fight, not listening. You trust that whatever it is, it makes sense for her, even though you might not understand it yet. So, you 1) Evaluate the situation. Find out whether it is as simple as fixing her low blood sugar or deeper than that. 2) Make yourself available. You eliminate all distractions and get curious about her challenge. 3) Put on your coaching hat. You assume the position of a coach and utilize an array of tools to support her through it. 4) Offer a safe space. You make sure that the only thing you bring to the

109

scene is unconditional love and leave judgment at the door. This leads us to Step 5) Wait for the first move. After you've created a safe space for your child as she goes through a highly emotional moment, wait for her to make the first move. This gives her the opportunity to fully experience her emotions so she can release them and watch them move out of her body and space. Ignore time at this point because this is ultimately about her transformation.

Remember when you were a teenager learning to drive? You had to constantly check the rearview mirror and the side mirrors. You were trying to find a comfortable way to hold the steering wheel. Getting the car to move wasn't too bad, but learning to brake without jerking your body to and fro was another story. Ah, watch out! It took all your conscious attention to make sure you weren't going to run over a squirrel. Whew, it was just a twig. It was nerve-racking and took every ounce of focus you could give. Now that you've been driving for years, have you ever taken a long-distance drive and made it for 15 minutes or an hour without realizing how it happened? It's like you wound up in your driveway and the last thing you remembered you were miles away? That's because you've mastered the skill of driving to the point that it doesn't require your full, conscious attention. It has been relegated to the subconscious mind, just like breathing and brushing your teeth. It frees up 10 percent of the conscious mind to focus on learning new information. This leaves the majority of your decisions in life to be made by your subconscious mind.

Knowing how the conscious and subconscious minds play a role in your life is critical information. If you don't know what lurks beneath the surface, you might not like what shows up in your life experience. This is a pivotal point because your child is getting her programs in these early years. They will be stored and filed in her subconscious mind as the driver and library of reference points to guide her life decisions. It's a big responsibility for you, but don't let the weight of that scare you. I shed light on this functionality so the awareness will affect your conscious decisions in how you choose to coach her through life. Are there moments that are draining, exhausting, and challenging for you? Yes, they can be at times, especially when it's been several days or weeks of the same thing at peak levels sending waves of unrest through the whole family system. Yes, that is hard. Some of it is age appropriate. Some of it is because she is learning how to maintain her own energy. Other parts are because she needs your leadership to coach her through the darkest moments a child can have. When she's in the midst of a breakdown, can you sympathize by remembering your last adult breakdown? You have more tools than she does, and still, it was really uncomfortable while you were working your way through the muck. Imagine how much harder it must be for her. She may be wise spiritually and intelligent in many ways for her age, but those precocious qualities she possesses can make you forget that she is a little human being learning how to be in this world. There are so many rules, so many regulations that are unsaid, unspoken, and uncommunicated. Oh my! No wonder she breaks down at times. It's overwhelming. This is especially the reason to wait for her to make the first move. Give her a chance to take it in, breathe, process, and make heads or tails out of it. Even if it's something you've repeated endless times, realize there is a valid reason she's not getting it. Try another way. When she has her next breakdown, be like Mister Rogers. Take off your normal jacket and shoes. Put them in the closet and hang up that outfit for the time being. Then, put on your cozy sweater of compassion, empathy, and understanding. Put on the shoes your coach-self would wear. Sit by her without expectation of outcome. Be sure to approach the situation and her body with respect to her as another human with her own set of lessons. The only thing you bring into the space is the blanket of unconditional love. Imagine there is a dome of energy large enough for both of you. Wherever she is, meet her there, physically, emotionally, spiritually, and psychologically. Take a deep inhale of light and ask for Source guidance. Then, step into the dome in a way that is receptive to her energy, non-invasive, and non-threatening. She is a person. She is not merely a child for your molding. She is a soul with her own mission and purpose. You are her human guide until she is ready to fly. When you remember that, gratitude, and appreciation rush in and therein begins the mending process.

We all live in our own model of the world. Imagine that each person has a bubble around their body and the way they perceive the world is through an invisible film. The film is like a filter through which everyone receives information from the world around them. Your mind is bombarded with millions of bits of information per second. So your brain doesn't crash like an overloaded computer, it has mechanisms to locate relevant information. The relevancy it filters for are created by programs it received during the early years of life. The programs are installed by the beliefs handed down from parents, teachers, media, advertisements, toys, news, conversations, and other sources of information. An example of a program is when a parent comes home stressed out about losing their job and, in a panic, shouts at the child, "Why did you break this! Money doesn't grow on trees, you know!" There was a logical explanation why the parent freaked out. The unintended and highly impactful outcome was that the child instantly received a program installed into her subconscious mind stating that money is really hard to come by. She may even make up another layer of story to say that she's not worthy of things she loves. Humans, no matter the age, have a computer-like brain that receives input, categorizes information for relevancy, and makes up wild stories to fill in any gaps to make sense of this big, confusing world. With millions of bits of information being thrown at you every second of your life, your mind must have a way to filter out what doesn't apply for your survival's sake. If it is irrelevant, then it gets trashed. It won't even enter your conscious mind. It all happens subconsciously in the blink of an eye without your conscious awareness. So much happens as a reaction without conscious decision. If her first move doesn't fit in with the mold of acceptable behaviors, then take a deep breath and peel back the layers to find out what's really going on beneath the surface.

When children are taught to make choices based on what other people may think, they are taught to give away their power. There are times when a child's big emotions trigger your own unprocessed emotions of the past. It happens so quickly without thought. The reaction brings up agitation, annoyance, and impatience. It's uncomfortable to watch someone experience raw pain. When children are told to handle it when they are in the midst of an emotional breakdown, because the adult can't handle the trigger, then the child is essentially told to swallow the undigested pain and put a lid on it. If the adult doesn't teach her how to process this tangled mess of confusing emotions, how will she ever learn to authentically know what emotions are and how to deal with them? If she is so far removed from understanding her own inner workings, how will she ever know the difference between her own feelings and those of others? How will she learn to use her internal GPS called intuition and discernment if she is consistently told to override her instincts? When will she get the opportunity to develop the important skill of emotional intelligence? *Sorry baby, you will have to wait, pile up all your unprocessed emotions for 30-plus years until you have a mental breakdown and seek the help of a specialist, like me.* This is why I developed the Light Warrior School and empowerment programs for children. I was that person who suppressed my traumas until I had a mental breakdown just before turning 30. I cried for literally 365 days. It put me straight onto the path of self-development and spiritual expansion. It helped me find my dharma to fulfill my soul purpose. It made me deeply committed to helping others build their version of heaven. So, as I spent more than 10 years helping women overcome and reprogram their adult mind and heal the inner child, it struck me that giving these tools to children early on would serve them their entire lives too. The ripple effect would send waves of empowering impact into the lives of her friends, family, future partners, and work relationships. When she reaches adulthood, she would have reached a level of mastery by practicing these tools for well over 10,000 hours. Her children and the generations after that will benefit exponentially. This is where change really begins. It starts with the individual until we reach the tipping point of the 100th monkey effect where the entire globe enjoys a transformational paradigm shift.

Every moment of every day holds the power of a teaching moment. Weaving the knowledge seamlessly into daily life allows it to penetrate your child's mind with ease and grace. Even in the midst of leading her, remember to allow her the space of individualized expansion and exploration. Let her discover her inner workings and respond when she's ready. To honor her is to set the tone of how she will teach others to treat her. Model it, be it vibrationally, in your thoughts, in your being-ness, actions, choices, and interactions with others. You are emanating messages non-stop and she is picking this up. Learn it, embody it, then show her the daily practice of how to: 1) ground into Earth energy, 2) keep a bubble of protection on, and 3) connect to Source energy. This is the foundation to keeping your energy integrity intact while living in this world. If your energy is compromised, it weakens your ability to lead a happy, healthy, and abundant life. If you're scrambling to survive, how will you ever thrive? If you're focused on fixing the sadness, illness, or paying the bills, how will you rise into the power position to lead your family and child? Yes, challenges show up from time to time. Channel your inner superhero who has the power to see it coming, the faith to filter for its inherent gift, and conviction to live it every day. Chose to be the one who overcomes. Chose to get up again and again. This is why you came. So, bring it!

Every morning, you can speak an affirmation aloud to model your practice. For instance, "I'm going to have a great today. How about you?" If your energy is high and full of joy, she will naturally want to be there, too. So much in life is about energy management. When I speak from the stage, I am in tune with the energy of the audience as a whole organism. When I'm running the school full of children, I am managing and reading the energetic needs of the entire group. When I practice *feng shui* in my home, I am managing the flow of energy in the physical space to nourish all the areas of our lives from money to sex, from love to reputation. When I am coaching a client, I am feeling her energy and tuning into what would serve her highest good, even over the phone. Waiting for her to make the first move is exactly that. You are managing the energy of the dynamic between the two of you.

If you woke up on the wrong side of the bed and can't authentically say you're doing awesome, then please don't. If you say an affirmation that you are not in a vibrational match with, it would be a lie. The mismatch in vibration is confusing and intuitively your child will know you are out of alignment. In this way, you are teaching her that it's not OK to be upset and, if you are, that you need to lie and cover it up because it's not OK to be your authentic self. What you can do first is to lean on your energetic practices to get back in alignment. Meditate, breathe, call in the angels to help you out, grab a crystal that transmutes negative energy, pray, go for a walk in nature, journal, or call a friend. Or you can even lock the bathroom door and shed a tear. Better yet, find a sitter to watch the kids and take care of yourself for a couple hours. Do what you've got to do to get there. There's no judgment. Just do it. Then, you can lead effectively for the highest good. Leaders can only lead when they are already at the desired point. And what she needs from you as a leader is someone who can hold the space for her transformation without rushing her to an end result.

If you're having a tough day, you can be honest and use it as a teaching moment. There's no need to burden her with the details of your challenge. The point is to share the process in how you deal with the challenging emotions you're experiencing. Be like a news anchor and broadcast what you're doing because it will indirectly explain what you're doing and why. Say, *"I'm having a really challenging day today, but I know I can feel better. I'm going to take a deep breath in until I can't anymore and I'm going to hold it for as long as I can before letting it out slowly."* She'll probably be so curious about mommy holding her breath that she'll stick around to watch. Right there, you are programming her with the belief that there might be hard days and that's OK. She'll see that no one is perfect, not even mom. And when she has a challenging day, there are ways to feel better. After a few rounds of intentional breathing, your whole mind, body, and spirit system will feel relief, allowing the vibration in your being to rise. All at once, you've modeled what it means to have self-acceptance, self-love, self-care, authentic communication, self-leadership, and self-compassion. Too often, women want to be the best mom possible by giving themselves completely. Then, this plan backfires when she overgives by not honoring her own needs and she loses herself in the process. That's how women subconsciously pass down the self-defeating belief that to be a great mom, we must give until our tank is empty. When you model this ability to love yourself through the hardship and accept what is by breathing it out, she will have that as a powerful reference point the next time she's having a really hard day.

Children's breakdowns can occur for so many reasons. It can be obvious and immediate or it can be pent-up feelings of fear and being scared of things they don't understand. When Daddy has to go to work although she wants him to stay, this can make her feel out of control of her life and environment. One day, she will understand the other side of the equation, but for now, she has to swallow the discomfort day after day and find a way to process it. If there is no outlet, eventually, when enough little challenges have piled up, the tiniest incongruency will break her shell and every emotion will come tumbling out without control. To someone who doesn't know this yet, she could be standing there in shock wondering why her child is crying over the cereal, when in fact, the cereal issue was simply the last straw that cracked open the water dam. What can be done in those situations? Wait for her. Give her space. Allow her to be. Here are a few steps to follow:

1. Compassion: Remember how scary these big emotions are, especially for little people.

2. Energetic Safety: Put a large energy dome over the space where she is.

3. Love: Take a deep breath in from Source and breathe it out. Intentionally direct a stream of pink, unconditional love into the dome.

4. Alignment: Put on the bubble, ground into the Earth, connect yourself to Source.

5. Intention: Non-judgment, effective listening, holding the space.

6. Enter: Now you can enter the dome because you're in alignment and have set up the energetic support for everyone involved.

7. Presence: Simply be present to her pain holding the vision that she is capable of making it to the other side. See in your mind that she is whole and well.

8. Boundaries: It's OK for her to scream, kick, or punch a pillow. It's OK to go outdoors and throw a ball or something. Art, painting, drawing, and running are all great ways to let it out, too. It's OK to find a productive way to get the emotions out because the last thing you want is to get it all pent-up again. With that said, it's OK to do all those things as long as it doesn't hurt her, other people, animals, or her surroundings. You may need to repeat this firmly with love. Your goal is to find a physical space where she is safe to let the steam out without hurting anyone, anything, or herself. In these cases, don't look at the clock. It's irrelevant. If it's been pent-up for a while, it'll take a significant amount of time to get it out. What if

you had the chance to learn these tools to take care of yourself at that age? Would it help you now as an adult when emotional upsets occur? Let's give them a head start in this world.

Remember in Chapter 1 when we said, if your good friend calls crying on the phone, how would you handle it? You'd probably stop what you're doing and want to know what happened. This is the level of curiosity to offer a hurting child. Come into the interaction holding the space like a container of peace and love. When someone is scared and vibrating low, their energy and being is contracting. She's closing up. Therefore, holding a space open for her to emote and let it out without judgment is in itself extremely healing. As you hold her in the energetic space of love and understanding, seek first to understand. *I can see that you're feeling really sad/mad/ disappointed/scared/upset. Is there something I can do to help you feel better?* Then be quiet. You may offer her support from time to time, but really follow her lead and allow her to make the first move. Tune into her energy and what her needs might be. Sometimes she doesn't want to be fixed. Sometimes she just needs a good cry. Other times, after a good cry, she begins to open up and even gain clarity herself. She's still learning how to give words to feelings. Within each type of feeling, there are gradations and nuances that may not have words. Not having the clarity within herself and not having the ability to communicate certain feelings has got to be enormously frustrating. Whatever transpires is perfect. Just love her, remember that it's scary for her, and hold the vision of her getting the clarity she needs to move on. When you have trust on that level, she will learn to have that trust in herself, too. You are a masterful queen who rules with the power of majesty, equanimity, and foresight. A master is someone who doesn't speak until it is the exact time to speak. Wait for her to come through the other end.

As with any story, there is a beginning, middle, and end. The emotional breakdown will have a similar arc. When the crying slows down, the intensity tapers off and the breathing normalizes, these are all signs that the climax has passed. You can initiate some slow deep breaths for yourself so she may sync up with you. You can offer a hug because she might be more open to it now that the feelings have passed through her body. If she isn't ready, let her know it's totally OK and that you are there when she's ready. If she comes in for a hug, be that rock, and love on her. Embrace her and give her empowering, uplifting words of encouragement. Comfort her. You are her coach in the boxing ring. Let her know how well she did. It was hard, and she did it. Review in a few short phrases what just happened. *"I love you baby. You did it. Did you see how that yucky energy was all in your body making you feel bad? And if you don't hold onto it, eventually it will pass through you? You did it. You let it pass through you. You're safe. And you are so loved. Well done, baby."* It's not easy being a young human feeling so many big feelings and not knowing how to make sense of it all. This will set a self-empowering reference point for your child as she grows into an emotionally intelligent adult.

A lot of what you're doing when you're coaching your child through an emotional challenge is simply holding the space with unconditional love. Listen like a good friend, and offer a hug or support when needed. Sit nearby waiting to be called. Be patient and simply be the witness to the birthing of a child going through her own metamorphosis. This is a journey of a lifetime. There is no rush to be anything other than who she is here to be: a conscious, confident, and connected child.

CHAPTER 9

Step 6:
Elevate the Vibrational Energy

*"What you do every day matters more
than what you do once in a while."*
–Gretchen Rubin

You're doing awesome! By this point, you've really made your child's emotional challenge and transformation a priority. You're in the energetic dome together and you're waiting for her to make the first move. You're holding the sacred space for her to experience these big emotions, to learn how to make sense of everything while finding a way to move through it in a healthy manner. As you take the stance as a witness and patient coach, you can quietly elevate the energy of the space to support the process. The breath of unconditional love is a great technique. You can call in the angels to assist you with greater ease and grace. Holding the vision of a peaceful conclusion pulls that reality into existence. Trusting that everything is unfolding in divine perfection welcomes that into your experience. Pulling in universal love to heal the situation helps. Cleansing the space, praying, and breathing are all ways to elevate the energy.

We are alive in very exciting times. More and more people are waking up from the slumber, however, there is still much work to be done and the Universe is calling on you. It's calling on all of us to raise our minds and hearts to catch the inspiration from Source. It's shining the light on everyone's consciousness and lifting the veil. Source is tapping you on the shoulder. It's asking you to stand up now and show yourself unapologetically. If you realize your greater role in the grand scheme of life, in humanity's evolution and its chance to transcend from a world dominated by fear to one attuned to love, then raise your hand. If you know that change is possible and have seen the vision, then you must spread the light. You are the warrior who came to hold the channels open for the next generation to run through and take our collective evolution to the next level. You've worked so hard to withstand being the black sheep. You were brave enough to carve out the path you knew was for the highest good, even in the face of rejection. You felt the congruence of staying true to who you really are – a divine being here to be a representative of the light. You are an agent of love. Now you get to pass on your wisdom and knowledge to the next generation so the whole world may benefit.

If you've ever been on an airplane, you're familiar with the emergency instructions. In fact, the instructions clearly direct adults to put on their oxygen mask first, before helping children and elderly. Why? Well, if the strongest and most capable people take care of themselves, then they are available to help the small and weak. It is imperative that the ones most able to care for the injured are alive and well. This serves the highest good for everyone aboard the plane. You are that person. You are the one who has seen the light, who recognizes the truth, who is inspired by transformation, and who is awakened to a life of expanding consciousness. Once you realize this, there's no going back. The only way is onward and upward, and you're bringing the crowd with you. If you don't take care of yourself first, then the part of the mission you took on will not last. If you understand the critical value of your role, then you will know that nurturing yourself to a state of wholeness is non-negotiable. We need your presence and leadership. Your contribution is indispensable. Without your conscious leadership at the helm of your family's life, who will shine the light on the pathway? If you've seen the light and are inspired by the greatness within, then hear this: In order for you to keep up with Source, you have to take care of your body. Otherwise, you'll pass out from exhaustion and miss out on all that you came to do.

Filling your energy tank to overflow is the goal. Giving from overflow serves from the highest degree. It was so easy before you were married and had kids. Single ladies go for a massage, meet up with girlfriends, go to the gym and do whatever her mind, body, or spirit requested. Then, as soon as motherhood arrived, everything changed. Too many moms give up their identity and lose themselves in their new role. You never intended to be a martyr, but that's what happened when your tank slipped quietly into the red. Wanting to be the best mom possible, you gave every ounce of your energy to nurture your child. In the blink of an eye, two years passed and you felt run down, haggard, and totally depleted. It feels like you've been running a marathon without rest or water. Showering and using the toilet uninterrupted sounds like a dream. You wish you could stop feeling guilty and give your body the massage it has been screaming for. It would be amazing not to feel like everyone is vying for your attention or pulling you in 20 different directions. Everyone wants something from you and, at this point, there is barely any energy left. Operating from an empty fuel tank for years, you see that your account is in the negative and you owe yourself buckets of self-care. Steps from depression and staring in the face of a potential breakdown, you might feel alone and exhausted, yet so badly you want to be the perfect mom. No one told you that didn't exist, except in the fabricated stories of your mind.

The inner critic whips you into submission each day. "Do this, do that. You're not doing enough. You're not good enough." It shouts incessantly. Ahhh! Oh no! You finally break and burst at the seams. Luckily, this isn't as terrible a place as it may seem. Emotional breakdowns are powerful because now you're open to change. You can finally hit the reset button and rebuild yourself with intention. You know what doesn't work. Trying so hard to be this unattainable person doesn't work. Clarity about what you do want arises out of the pain. Great! It is the incentive never to go there again. Declaring that you will take care of yourself, you claim your worth and slowly strengthen the muscle of carving out time and space to feed the mind, body, and spirit. At once, you throw guilt into the fire and stand tall knowing that, to be the best mom possible, you must first fill your tank to overflowing. Knowing the implications of modeling this for your daughter, you are empowered finally to shift the perspective and you know that every choice and action shows your daughter what is possible as a woman. It reinforces that the pathway is wide open for future generations to run forth into the world with the torch of enlightenment blazing unabashedly into the leading edge – moms who have the courage to stand up and give their daughters permission to take it even further into the unknown. You are a pioneer leading the way as a change agent. For that big role, you will need a tank full of energy.

There is another voice within that is your best ally. Have you ever noticed that still small voice inside talking to you? It exists for everyone. The more you pay attention to the whisper, the louder it will grow. You have the ability to turn up the volume. How cool is that? We are all born with the tool of intuition and discernment. It is the connection to your soul, Source, and higher self. That little voice will never make you wrong, blame, shame, or make you feel bad. That negative voice accompanied by the whip is something else completely. It is usually the voice of your parent or other authority figure judging you from the past. Take a listen next time and find out whose voice it sounds like. Don't let that run your life. Recognize it, acknowledge it, then watch it move out of your mind and space. Resisting it will only feed it and make it stronger. Instead of putting up a fight and allowing more conflict to grow, imagine sidestepping it to let it fall right past you. The negative voice in your head doesn't serve you; it's an old program running in your subconscious mind, like an old, broken record. Aren't you sick of listening to the same garbled song over and over again? It's time to delete it, girl! Ready! Imagine that song on the playlist stored in your memory bank. Now press the delete button and watch the file disappear completely. It's gone! It's not even in the trash bin. It got fully deleted automatically. Take a deep breath. Then, feel how good it feels not to have that running your life anymore. Every time you experience that negative policing in your mind, delete it! The negative energy vibrates lower than an affirming thought. So, grab that thought and send it into the fire. Burn it, release it, let it go! Hear it sizzle in the flames. Watch the smoke dissipate into thin air. Then, intentionally put in a new program. What do you want instead? If you let go of fear, then affirm love. If you released judgment, then invite unconditional acceptance. It's important to fill the newly-created space with something empowering, otherwise it will be filled with whatever is floating in the ethers. Once you've re-programmed yourself, feel the relief in your body as it relaxes a bit. You are the authority of your life. It's time to take stock, clear house, and intentionally keep the empowering programs in your space. Regularly practicing this elevates your vibration and shakes off the false beliefs you've been holding onto. This is how you can be your true, powerful self. Anything less simply has to go.

Cleaning up the old garbage that's been hiding in the shadows of the subconscious mind is an ongoing exercise. The moment the prey stops being aware is the instant the panther eats it alive. Turn the tables. Be the panther – vigilant and poised. As the old gets cleared out, space is created for flow to pour into your life. What is the flow? Flow is when you're tuned into Source. It's when you have allowed yourself to be a vehicle for the light to work through. It is felt when you get out of your own way and let the life force move through you. Imagine that you have an energy tank that is used to run your life. When it is full and overflowing, life is amazing. It flows without effort. You feel like you're dancing through life; there's more than enough time to get all your tasks completed and all your relationships are flourishing with ease and grace. It's heavenly! When the fuel tank is on empty, however, and you're still giving as if your tank were full, what happens? It is a nightmare. You're stressed out and the day seems to be filled with roadblocks and challenges every step of the way. Your anxiety infects like a virus to others in your life and the domino effect falls into your path. Crawling back into bed sounds like a great idea, except that you have things to do and people to care for. What now? Just pause. Press the stop button. Take a deep cleansing breath and be OK with what is in that very moment. Whatever it is, it's OK and it's going to be OK. You've gone through tough situations before and you're still alive. Accept the pain of it all, as it is, for a brief moment. Everything is transient, just like a breath. It will pass, but it requires your awareness. Once you are conscious again, then you can easily take steps to get back in alignment with the flow.

How can you consciously get yourself back in alignment? Great question! There are infinite ways and there's no one right way or wrong way. When it comes to figuring out how to fill up your energy tank, there are a few categories to consider. Let's do this together. Take out a sheet of paper or open your journal. Make four columns with these titles: 1) Mind, 2) Body, 3) Spirit, and 4) Space. To be a whole and healthy person, these four areas need to be nurtured and nourished. In a moment, we'll be filling in each column with daily practices you'll want to implement.

Your mind is like the computer of your life. What you input will output as life experiences. The quality of information you allow into your mind is the direct connection to the quality of your life. If there are parts of your life you're not loving so much, no worries! Reverse engineer it. Identify what you want to alter, go back to the drawing board and find out what it is you want instead. Put more of those kinds of messages into your mind. How? Your mind processes information as images, sounds, feelings, sensations, scents, and internal dialogue. Taking the time each day to intentionally program your mind for exactly what you want to create is a way to become the master of your life. Read uplifting books and those that teach you how to strengthen your mind. Leaders are readers. Commit every day to reading at least five pages of a book that will make you a better person. Listen to music that pumps you up and elevates your mood. As the song raises your vibration, it will be good for your health and emanate everywhere around you. Post affirmations on your bathroom mirror so you are sure to see them every day. Starting the morning by feeding your mind with the powerful affirmations of love, abundance, and joy will attract more of these things into your life with ease and grace. It will draw in these qualities like filings to a magnet. When you lie in bed at night, spend those 10 minutes before drifting off to purposefully use your imagination as a creator would. Since the subconscious mind doesn't know the difference between what's real and imagined, you can use that to your advantage. Just like an Olympian or an astronaut who spends hours practicing precise moves and procedures in her mind, you can do this too. Program your mental computer in the coding language it understands: visual, auditory, kinesthetic, or auditory digital (self-talk). Create the movie of what you want to live and step right into the scene. Look around. What do you see with your eyes? Where are you? Notice the colors, sounds, people, view, temperature, dialogue, and energy. Note as many details as you can, as if you were right there. Who's there? Are they saying anything? Turn up the volume, the colors, the sensations. Feel it all running through your body. Enjoy what it feels like to live the life you've always wanted. Now stay there in the vibration of all that juicy goodness until you drift off to sleep with a smile on your face. Do this every night. Do it first thing in the morning before getting out of bed. This exercise informs your mind what kind of life you are living already. This is when you are ruling your domain from the throne. Your mind is waiting for your direction. You, the inner presence, are the director of this life and much of it starts here in the realm of thoughts, feelings, and images. On your sheet of paper with the four columns, list specific daily practices you want to implement to program your mind. Write as many ideas as your mind produces. Don't filter or judge. Let it all come out. Once the list feels complete, we will move onto the next section.

This mental mastery tool is something you can do easily with your child. Take her through a guided meditation leading her through an empowering theme relevant to her current situation. If she wants to make a goal in her next soccer game, teach her how to practice in her mind that winning shot. If she scores and wins her next game, connect it back to this mental practice. Explain to her how powerful the mind is and the process of how thoughts are things. When she thinks positive thoughts, she elevates her vibration and attracts more of this energy. When she thinks self-defeating and negative thoughts, she attracts more of that too. Here's another way to teach children the concept that thoughts are things. When my oldest daughter was three learning to lose gracefully at board games, I used this very lesson to help her expand her mind. When she wasn't getting ahead on the board game, her mood quickly disintegrated and her attitude and facial expressions exposed negative self-talk she was having in her own mind. She was probably thinking, *"I'm never going to win. I'm not good enough. I'm dumb. I hate this."* Rather than scold her and make her feel wrong, I encouraged her by sharing this idea. I told her that what she thinks about comes about. I explained that when she thinks happy thoughts, she will begin to get ahead. Therefore, when she thinks thoughts that make her feel bad, she will fall behind. When she got the message, her face lit up! She was excited to know that there was a trick and a method to winning. With renewed energy, she dove right back into the game and actually won. It's an excellent way for children to practice and connect the mental and physical worlds together. Try it and have fun. Keep it light and curious. Fast-forward two years and I hear her tell others, *"If you believe it, it will be."* So true! I love having these little people reflect the truth back to the community, and so will you. This is an empowered child planted with the seeds of conscious leadership. Imagine a generation of empowered children ruling the world.

Moving onto the next area, let's take a look at this incredible body as your brilliant vehicle. It is a sacred space because it houses the spirit, your soul, the extension of the light from the greater powers that be. Without this body, the soul would not have the chance to experience this life as you, with this name and this face. It's like a car. Imagine your body is a Rolls Royce. Would you polish it often, give it gas, get it washed, make sure it's well-oiled, and well taken care of? Of course! It's amazing to have a beautiful machine that will take you from point A to point B whenever you ask it to. It allows you to interact with people and objects to create new ideas and fulfill personal desires. It's quite amazing if you think about it. So, why do people abuse it so frequently? By abuse, I mean those times when you don't rest, don't eat properly, don't give it the maintenance it requires to continue being a well-run machine. It is here to serve you. As the mind serves you like a computer, the body serves you as the Rolls Royce. You are the queen. What are all the ways you can take utmost care of this vehicle? Giving it the clean nutrients and fluids it requires. Getting into bed by 10 p.m. allows your organs to regenerate themselves. Spending time in bare feet, earthing on a patch of grass will rebalance your positive and negative ions with the Earth. This reduces inflammation, which is the root of numerous illnesses, like heart disease and arthritis. Try the Japanese practice of forest bathing by strolling among the trees. Going to the ocean and breathing in the life-supporting negative ions in the sea breeze is cleansing and relaxing. Take a salt bath in your tub to bring a sense of calm. Move your body each day in simple exercise to strengthen the vehicle and lift your spirits. Look into tai chi, qi gong, and yoga. These practices keep your mind clear and cultivate the life force in your body. Eating foods that are non-genetically modified (non-GMO), devoid of chemicals, toxins, and preservatives will keep your machine running smoother and cleaner, able to hold more light. If you're a Rolls Royce, would you feed it discount gas or top-of-the-line fuel, perhaps hydrogen or solar (if it were compatible)? Your body is a highly-prized vehicle. The window of opportunity for a sperm to successfully fertilize an egg is mind-blowingly miniscule. You are here because one in a million sperms made it to one healthy egg. For that reason, you are priceless by nature. How amazing are you! So, take care of your vehicle. Pull out your paper and write down as many things as you can that you can do to take care of your body. Write down your favorite ways to nourish your physical self. Don't be shy, you're the only one looking at this list. Treating your body like a prized vehicle and sacred temple elevates its vibration and energy. The more areas of your life that are operating well to overflow, the easier it is to notice what is out of balance. You could quickly assess a systems check on all of the categories of your life and know what needs tending and what parts are running smoothly. There are many moving parts, but it's totally doable to systemize yourself so it becomes a habitual practice to elevate yourself in every way. Life will be more fun and enjoyable because the feeling tone of your daily experience will be one of health, vitality, and well being.

Next, let's take a look at nurturing your spirit. What makes your heart sing? What brings out the kid in you? What makes you smile so much your face hurts? What tickles your insides till you giggle out loud? Put on some loud music and dance around like crazy. Shake that booty! Be silly until your kids are laughing and you're cracking up, too. Get some paints out and make something abstract. Feel the energy come from your heart and out through your hands. Color in a coloring book. Write poetry, make a journal entry, or write a love letter to yourself. Stick your hands into the dirt as you plant some flowers and feel how good it is to have the dirt all up under your nails. Lay on the grass and look up at the sky searching for cloud animals. Skip around like a kid. Oh yes! Why are our kids so free and happy? They have no cares. They are in the flow. They are still living from the connection they have with Source. They simply live in joy, feel deeply, and stay present to the moment. This is where adults can learn so much from the young. This next one is a must. Meditate daily. The more you sit, the easier it is to drop right into the sacred chambers where the soul resides waiting to meet with you each day. It delights in your presence and rejoices in your conscious partnership. It is powerful, not forceful. It is nourishing and rejuvenating. It is an automatic reset and a way to find peace and fulfillment. Collaborating with your inner self is the ultimate path to great illumination. Now, take out your paper once again. List all the ways you can feed the connection to your soul. Don't filter, simply let it flow. The more time you spend connecting with your inner self, the stronger the communication line. This inner presence is the same as the infinite Source energy that is everywhere and in everything. Closing your eyes, breathing in, and entering your soul space in your heart area is all you need to do to spend some quality time with yourself. This is the space where you increase your intuition, inner guidance, knowledge, and awareness. It is the seat of your soul. The goal is to practice this connection to the point that every moment of every day is driven from this place. Eventually, with persistence, you will feel fully guided in all that you do in this life. The exact people, places, and opportunities will present at the right time. The things and situations to serve your highest good will unfold with greater ease. Surrender to the power of your heart and soul and enjoy the flow of life living as you.

Children naturally love all the things that would elevate this category. All you have to do is create more time and space to play, be creative, and let the spirit flow freely. When it comes to the quiet meditative practices, use this book. Go on a slow walking meditation in nature with the directions to pay attention to every tiny detail. Sit outdoors without conversation and teach her to choose one spot to gently focus on with her eyes while breathing life in deeply. She can also close her eyes and focus on slowly inhaling to the count of five, pause, and exhale to the count of six. These are simple ways to lay the foundation of maintaining her connection to the inner presence. These practices will elevate both of your vibrational energies and support the evolution of your lives.

Lastly, we have the category of space. *Feng shui* is the art of managing the energy in your environment. It is an incredible tool of empowerment if you understand how to use it to your advantage. Without getting deeply into it, you can still benefit from knowing some basic tools. Since everything is energy, it makes sense to treat the environment we work and live in with the same level of intention and awareness. The number one offender in *feng shui* is clutter. You must have a consistent lifestyle of decluttering. Purge, release, and let go. Those items you are hiding and hoarding in the attic hold unprocessed emotions and issues you have not consciously faced within. Be brave, take the time, ask a friend to sit with you, whatever you need. Do it. Go into the basement and sort things out. Look everywhere from the junk drawer to the closet. The garage to the side yard. Oh yes, it's not just your living space, it's your entire property – even your wallet and underwear drawer. Get in there, girl. Look at it. If you can't decide immediately to toss or keep, feel into it. Ask yourself, *"Does it nurture me to keep it?"* If you haven't opened those boxes in two years or worn that dress in three years, let it go. You'll make space for something of higher vibration. See it as a way to upgrade your life in all areas. Holding on to something due to an unconscious fear of lack will attract more of the same depleting energy. Holding onto the past sabotages you. It keeps you from enjoying the present and prevents you from creating the future you desire. That clutter is a reflection of your inner state. The good news is, once you clear the junk externally, the junk will begin to clear internally. It's a two-way street. Another tool is to fix anything that is broken in the house. If you can't fix it, get rid of it.

The energy of something that is broken, and never going to be used is decay and stagnant. The energy that doesn't move collects more of the same life-depleting force. You don't want that in your space especially if you're attempting to increase your life force. Cultivate a practice of being in tune with your home environment. The more you practice that energetic connection, the more automatic it becomes. How can you upgrade your life? Let it all go so more elevating life force energy can come in and nurture all areas of your family's life.

Once you've cleared your space, now you can add things intentionally. Adding potted or artificial plants around the home will lift the vibration of your space. Removing images and gifts from ex-partners, ex-lovers, and ex-friends will instantly upgrade the energy. There is no need to have constant reminders and objects carrying the vibration of the past. It is possible to find gratitude, honor it for the lessons provided and bless it as you let it go to make space for better. Adding images that make you feel full, grateful, loved, and peaceful will support your mood every day. Choosing to allow only items that light you up is a subtle, yet powerful, way to program your unconscious mind for success, happiness, and health. Everything around you is sending subliminal messages to your mind at all times. Be intentional by taking away what doesn't serve. Then, design your empowering environment with purpose. You'll see a dramatic shift in your life experience. There's one last column on your paper. List all the things you can do to improve your space at home and at the office. To involve your child, begin with her own space. Regularly purge her bedroom and play area by doing the process with her. Go through each item and ask her if it something to keep or give away. If she wants to keep everything, explain that letting go makes room for better things to come in. You can point out which things are old, broken, or ready to be released. To help her make these decisions, ask her when she used it last. Teaching her the steps to purging on a regular basis will support her energetic and vibrational management on her own some day.

Now that you've created four beautiful lists of ways to nourish your mind, body, spirit, and space, I want you to circle the top three methods that call to you from each list. Identify the top three ways to nurture each part of yourself: mind, body, spirit, and space for a total of 12 items. You'll have the full long list in your possession forever. You can add, subtract and edit as the years go on. For now, take your top three favorite practices per category and write them neatly on an index card. This is a reference card you will look at every morning as a reminder of what you will do to fill your own tank. It is not a report card and not there to remind you of what you didn't do. Let it serve as a loving encouragement of the goals you are working toward. Write the items in order of preference. For example, MIND: 1) first favorite, 2) second favorite, 3) third favorite. Then, repeat for each category. Starting now you're going to pick one thing to practice per day. Rather than doing it all at once (which can be overwhelming and not sustainable), you will start slow. When you feel like that single practice is starting to take root in your daily routine, you add another practice. Practice those two new ways of self-care until they both feel like they are integrating into your daily life as habit, then add the third practice and so on you'll go. A baby doesn't learn to run straight out of the womb. New ways of being and mastery of life come from patiently practicing what matters. Start today and keep going. If you falter, get up, and dust yourself off. Ask yourself what is one thing you can do today to get yourself back on the wagon. It's not about not falling; it's about choosing to get up again. Go get it, girl. You got this!

I'm going to let you in on the secret routines I do each day. Below are the daily practices I use to protect my energetic space. They allow me to hold an energetic boundary that is nourishing and permit me to be in the world but not of the world. It takes work to uphold a boundary that will keep its integrity. It isn't hard, but it takes effort, consistency, and awareness. The moment you reach your goal at the gym and decide to coast for a while because you look good is the moment you slip away from what you've achieved. The same goes for spiritual practice. When you're practicing, you feel great. That's the time to up your game and keep on going. Don't coast. If you do, that's OK, you'll feel it. It doesn't slip down all in one shot, so you might not notice it right away. By the time you do, it won't feel too good because you're so far from the stream of flow. All you have to do is ask yourself, "What is one thing I can do today to get me back in alignment with Source's flow?" Then do it. No judgment. Nothing. Just do it. Here are a few of my favorite daily practices that I do to elevate my energetic vibration. Enjoy!

- Balancing Between Heaven and Earth
  With eyes closed in meditation, imagine a hollow
  tube three-feet in diameter all the way around

your body. This tube begins at the base of your spine and extends all the way down into the center of the Earth. See it in a solid vibrant color. This grounding cord hooks into the core of the Earth to support, nurture, and hold you up. Just as it receives water from above ground to filter through the soil, it too absorbs all your energy through its layers to cleanse impurities. As you inhale deeply and exhale fully, gently allow gravity to pull all that no longer serves you out of your body and energetic space. Sit in gratitude to Mother Earth as she upholds you unconditionally and recycles the parts of you that no longer serve. That's the first part. Second, from the crown chakra at the top of your head, reach all the way up into the sky. Go up past the clouds, stars, and sun. Go past the solar system and as far as you can until you reach the edge of the universe. From there, at the edge where all creation begins, pull down that Source creative energy. Bring that energy in through the top of your head, down the back of your head, down the back of your spine until it reaches the base of your spine to meet with the grounding cord. Let the Source energy cleanse any energetic blockages you may have had and flush it down into the Earth to be recycled for the highest good. Let all the impurities stay down beneath the Earth and cycle 90 percent clean and pure Source energy back up the front of your spine until it shoots out the top of your head returning to the Universe. Each day you practice this routine, start by releasing the old grounding cord and letting it retract automatically into the Earth. Then, continue by sending a new grounding cord into the core and following with a connection to Source. This will clear your energetic bodies, bring healing, and establish a clear contact with Source. Everyone has the ability to communicate directly with the greater power. It is up to you to tune into the station.

• Program Your Cells

Once you've established a connection with Earth and Source, now you can call back all your energy and program it for your highest good. Imagine a large golden sun floating a foot above your head. This golden sun has a magnet in the middle with your name in golden letters. With this sun, call in all the energy you've left scattered around the Earth as you live, work, and go about your life. Everywhere you go, every person you see, a small piece of your energy remains there. Intend the attraction of all your energy back to your golden sun. See it thick like honey. Give it a bright vibrant color. It all comes flying back with ease and grace. Once your sun has expanded enough to accommodate all the energy coming back to center, you can program it with exactly what you want to create in your life. Do you want more peace, love, and joy? Or do you want more empowerment, confidence, and courage? How about more vision, community, and travel? Maybe more money, opportunities, and mentors? Whatever the case, enter that vibrational signature into the golden sun by seeing the words written in it. You can program it with as many things as you wish. When you are complete, open the bottom of the sun and drink the honey in through the crown of your head. Let it flow all the way down filling up your toes, ankles, legs, hips, torso, neck, and face until it spouts out the top of your head like a water fountain. As it does, the energy fills in the seven layers of your aura healing any energetic tears and sending all the debris from your space straight into the blue flame in the corner of the room. The alchemical flame is there anytime you need it. It will neutralize everything you put in there. Once your energetic bubble is cleansed, full of Source energy and programmed with intention, then it's time to put in the protection rose.

- Pink Protection Rose

  The pink rose is a flower of high vibration. It represents love, which also vibrates highly. In front of you, just beyond the outer layer of your aura, ask a protection rose to come to your aid. As it floats there, put a picture of your face right into the middle of the flower. Ask it to orbit around the outside of your bubble acting as a decoy intercepting all negative energies that may have entered your space. Watch it orbit around your aura and thank it for its protection. Each time you practice this, start by sending the old protection rose into the blue flame. You might notice if the old rose is tattered from use or still in good shape. Send it into the flame, then proceed with creating a new one.

- Prayer: Ring of Fire

  "In the name of, through the power, and by the word of Jesus Christ, a wall of living flames is built round about me, and I thank you for this great protection now." As you say this prayer aloud with conviction, imagine seeing, hearing, and feeling the wall of flames rise all around you. Leave enough space between you and the fire so you don't feel constricted. Know that the fire protects you from any negativity that may enter your space.

- Prayer: 360 Degrees with God

  Dear God,

  Please be to my right and to my left to protect me from evil.

  Please be in front and behind me to guide me down the right path that is in line with my Universal Divine plan.

  Please be above me and below me so your will may come through me and I may do your good work on this Earth.

Please be within me and fill me with your spirit, with your bright light, love, joy, compassion, understanding, and forgiveness.

Please be all around me, surround me with your golden sphere and protect me from all harm, malicious tongue, disease, delusion, depression, and allow me to attract positive love energies and keep all else at bay.

Thank you. And so it is. Amen. Amin. Amon.

- Prayer: Violet Flame

  I am the flame of violet fire. I am the purity that God desires. I am that I am.

These are a few of the steps I take for my daily spiritual practice. With that said, there are still some days that are easier or more challenging than others. There are so many variables that affect our state. The more areas we can fill up and balance out, the easier the task of identifying which areas might be off. Sometimes it's a major spiritual growth spurt, and it hurts. In those cases, when coaching myself just isn't cutting it, boy am I grateful I have a coach to lean on. We share the same type of language and dedication for self-development. Having someone to hold the space and guide you through to the other side is inspiring and priceless.

You are a powerful magician, did you know? Magic is conjured up by the use of speaking words into manifestation. Are you doing it with awareness? Most people don't realize the power they hold in their words. Every time they complain about something, they are attracting more of it into their lives. The results in life are the feedback loop to let you know the reality of who you're being in this world. Remember, there's no good or bad. Eventually, it can be fun, even when you are going through a spiritual growth spurt, a.k.a. an emotional breakthrough. When you practice long enough and make it your lifestyle, even in the midst of challenge, you will feel the gratitude for the lesson that comes with growth. Your faith in the process will grow. Your trust in yourself and the universe will keep you feeling safe even in the middle of unnerving change. Life is so good. It is here for us to play, learn, and grow. As Michael Beckwith loves to remind us, *"Life is always for you. It is never against you."* Trust in the good of the world and allow yourself to enter the flow of life.

When you are in the midst of a challenge, ask yourself these questions:

1. Why did I create this? (Meaning, why did your soul choose this experience?)

2. What's the lesson here for me? (Meaning, what is the soul lesson you chose before coming into this lifetime?)

3. What's the highest purpose of all this? (Meaning, how does this challenge and lesson serve the highest good of all?)

When you ask, the answers will come. Make sure to keep meditating, listening, and watching for those signs. They're everywhere all the time. As you clean off your filter, the answers appear with greater ease, grace, and speed.

When you are tired of going through the same story over and over again, use this awesome prayer. It has always come through for me.

"Dear Universe,

I am so ready to move on from this repetitive situation. Please help me learn the lesson once and for all so I may finally graduate to the next level and never repeat it again.

Love,

Me"

Listen for the clues, then go do it. Have the courage to take immediate action. It's that simple. Bam!

These are the tools I use each morning to set the tone and integrity of my energetic space. When you ensure your personal alignment with the Source energy, then you are better equipped to lead your child and family. That vibrational alignment also allows everyone you come in contact with the opportunity to attune to your frequency. Now you are the tuning fork elevating the energy everywhere you go.

CHAPTER 10

Step 7:
Review What Just Happened

*"Your soul doesn't care what you do
for a living – and when your life is
over, neither will you."*
–Neale Donald Walsch

This is the final step of the EMPOWER Method. After all is said and done, give your child a frame of reference for what just happened. Acknowledge her for what she just went through. Depending on her mood and attention span, you can summarize the steps of her transformation in a quick and easy way. This offers closure, a chance to understand what she just experienced and assurance that she is still loved even though it was ugly and uncomfortable. Give hugs, kisses, encouragement, and other positive reinforcements. If there were instances you wanted to guide differently, this is the time to point them out in a productive and constructive manner. For instance, you could say, *"That was a lot of big emotions you*

149

were processing. I noticed you might have felt angry. It's OK to have these feelings and learn to let them pass through your body. Next time, instead of kicking the plant because the pot can break and hurt your body, you can definitely kick the big body pillow as much as you want. Understand? I want to keep you and our home safe. And there are other ways you can get your mad out." This type of dialogue gives her permission to explore safe outlets for her emotions within the boundaries of safety.

Frame the experience in a way that guides her up the mental path of empowered thinking. Her mind is making connections between her outer and inner worlds. The neurology in her brain is creating stories and storing them in her subconscious mind for future reference. She's creating the software of her life-operating system. Help her by leading her away from any sense of self-judgment, blame, or shame. Empower her by shining the light of awareness on why the challenging moment served her in the long run. Point out the parts you want her to keep in her toolbox and leave the rest.

Once the storm has passed and she is calm and receptive, start by loving her unconditionally. There is no immediate need to talk about it or discuss the incident too much. Simply receiving her the way she is in an air of total acceptance and respect for the big work she just did is encouraging and supportive. As she regains an increased level of balance, groundedness, and presence, you can ask if she's OK. Be her caring guide and guardian angel checking in with how she's feeling. You will know if she's open to a discussion. Just as you wouldn't press the issue with your best friend, allow her the right to be where she is. See it as an opportunity to inspire her to a higher vantage point to gain a more positive perspective that serves. Serves what? To serve the ultimate goal of self-empowerment, enlightenment, and a deeper connection to life.

Being an awakened parent and practicing conscious parenting doesn't automatically mean all your problems disappear overnight. In fact, if these are new ways of being for you and the family, there will be a learning curve for everyone. The quickest way to be disappointed, give up, and throw in the towel to any new endeavor is to expect the results to be immediate like a one-pill wonder. Your child's body took nine months to develop before coming into this plane of existence. Learning to eat and walk took many more months and years. Therefore, learning to be more conscious as a parent to guide an awakened child takes concerted effort, awareness, and patience. Setting an expectation of curiosity, adventure, and trust will support the unfolding with greater fun, ease, and grace. Like all new practices, it takes time, effort, patience, and persistence. If this idea of coaching your child through her emotional breakdowns until she gains a breakthrough is new to the family, have a planning or informative conversation with your partner so everyone is on the same page. Discuss how every member of the family will show up differently: mentally, emotionally, and physically. If everyone is at wit's end and surrendering to a higher road, then there is an openness to try something new. If what you've been doing all these years is not getting you what you want, then you have to do something different. Communicate openly and lovingly from the throne of a queen. Set the expectation for your partner and the whole family. If they are not going to read the book and participate, then that means this is your area of expertise and you are the main leader in this domain. Everyone has their strengths and roles in a family, so just like a business partnership, let everyone do what they are naturally talented to do and leverage each other's strengths. There's no need for everyone to be excellent in everything. If both parents want to participate, that's amazing. If one parent is the main leader, then the other parent agrees to be the supporting role in parenting with everyone moving in the same direction of the philosophy. This prevents confusion for the child and family. If you are the leader, then be sure to set an expectation to your partner that this is not a one-pill wonder. They say the overnight success was ten years in the making. This is a life you are guiding together and it is a lifelong journey. Paint the vision of an empowered future and align both of you with a greater purpose of creating a better world together. That is the inspiration that will pull you forward as a family. Create a vision board or a list of words to remind you and keep the family aligned in challenging times. Weave the empowering values through your space, energetic practices, family routines, daily conversations, and in all ways possible. When all members on your ship are focused in one direction, magic happens.

As a review, here is a summary of the EMPOWER Method:

E: Evaluate the Situation. Did something happen in that moment? Has she eaten in the last two hours and is having low blood sugar? Did she have good quality sleep last night? Is there an age appropriate challenge she's learning through? Is she injured? Maybe the breakdown is due to months of pent-up, unprocessed emotions.

M: Make Yourself Available. Just like you would pause to listen to a crying friend on the phone, pause and make yourself available through your body, listening, and energy. Come down to her eye level. Listen with an open heart full of non-judgmental curiosity. Be fully present with your energy. Turn off the stove, mute the phone, turn off the music. Be here now.

P: Put on Your Coaching Hat. You wear many hats. During an emotional breakdown, remember to put on your coaching hat. There is no judgment or shaming. You are the person on higher ground who holds the vision for the child who's emotionally hurting to break through to the other side.

O: Offer a Safe Space. Physically make the space around her safer if she's having a physical tantrum and thrashing about. If she wants to punch and scream, then either make that space supportive of that action or bring her to a place that has soft components like pillows and blankets. Energetically, put on the dome, ground it, and connect it to Source energy. Repeat that for each body. Breathe in and out unconditional love through your soul space. Blanket the scene with love and compassion.

W: Wait for the First Move. After making your non-invasive, non-threatening presence available and known, wait for her lead. Bear witness to her process and watch to make sure her body stays safe. Bring the silent energy of readiness and support as you observe the arc from beginning to the end. Avoid counting the minutes because this will make it last forever. Drop into the present moment and breathe.

E: Elevate the Vibrational Energy. As you're serving her by holding the space as a witness, you can elevate the vibration of the scenario energetically. Call in the angels and unseen helpers. Pray for Source to show everyone the way. Fill the space with even more universal love. Use your mind's eye to pull out the negative energies from her or the space and throw it into a blue alchemical fire in the corner of the room. Negative energy isn't evil or scary. It simply is a vibratory level that registers lower on the scale of emotions. Keep it up as you hold space for her.

R: Review What Just Happened. Once the session has completed, naturally she will likely want to come in for a hug. Whether she does or not is OK. She just had an intense emotional breakthrough. She has transformed on some level internally. Give it a positive meaning for a learning point for future reference, and review what just happened in a few phrases that are also comforting and encouraging. For instance, it could be something like, *"Wow baby, that was hard work you just did. I'm so proud of you for letting the yuckies just pass through you instead of holding onto them."* Or, try: *"I love you baby. It's OK to feel those big, scary feelings. The best is to let it pass you just like you did so it doesn't stay inside. Good work."* It lets her know that she is loved, accepted, and seen, and everything is OK in her world.

When you take stock of the planet today, are you content with the state of world affairs? Do you feel like your existence has a positive and meaningful impact in the grand scheme of life for all? If not, what will you tell your child when she asks about all the injustices happening near and far? What will you tell yourself when it's time to leave Earth and you are passing the baton over to your child? Will you feel content on the level of participation you played in making a difference on this planet? What would you have wished you could do more of to leave her with a better world to raise your grandchildren and the next seven generations following?

This world is an incredible place. You chose to incarnate on Earth at this specific time in history for a purpose. As a soul family, you, your child, and all of the members made agreements to come into this lifetime together to play various roles for each other's opportunity to expand through soul lessons. Rather than spend 100 years of the common human lifespan running the hamster wheel to nowhere, it is possible to exit the cage of illusion and transform yourself from an externally programmed definition of success into an internally and Source guided path of empowerment. Take the steps to wake up, open the jail of your limiting beliefs, and fly free into the great expanse of infinite potentiality. You can reunite with your true essence as an emanation of the greater power, Source energy. Then, walk in this world without being controlled by the world. It all begins with the first step of awareness, conscious awakening, and ability to respond with intention.

The world may be reflecting an immense amount of deception, pain, and suffering caused by hidden agendas of an unloving nature. At the same time, the Earth also has an incredible amount of joy, beauty, and love woven into the fabric of our reality. Heaven and hell exist side by side differentiated only by your perception, attention, and focus. Cultivating an immutable strength through spiritual practice is the prerequisite for a fearless and courage-filled life. As of the writing of this book, the external world appears to be breaking down in every area of human existence. All around the world, people continue to be hungry, dying from drinking unhealthy water, starving from the lack of love, busied by the hustle and bustle of *making it*, whatever that means. In reality, you were born with the stream of Source energy pouring forth consistently within you all without effort. You are abundance in material form. The day you recognize this truth on a deeper level is the day you open yourself up to receive all that is yours from the beginning.

You exist. You are here, on Earth, in a body. This dense reality has the full range of truths and untruths. To wade through this heavy plane of dualistic information, you must cultivate the power of discernment to know what serves and doesn't serve you and the highest good of humanity. For when you gain the clarity from elevated consciousness, you are serving your child by showing her what's possible. You are leading the way. The first person to wake up in this game of illusions inherits the leadership position to shed light onto the path for all to find. Use your heart as a barometer. Heed the messages of your gut when it talks. Listen to your intuition as it is part of your internal guiding system. You have all the tools within you to wake up fully to the powerful divine presence that is you. You are it already. You are a bright light with the wisdom of the ages programmed from the divine. You are the light of Source, and it is the layers of erroneous beliefs you have agreed to that is covering any of it up. That is part of the game. Find out what those are and transform them into your greatest gifts. Once you take the time to face them and befriend what was once your dark side, you will find the power of shedding the light onto the shadow side and slay the monsters on the spot. The metamorphosis holds the catalytic energy of propelling you right into the next level of conscious development. This kind of authentic power can never be taken away from you, unless you agree to give it away. All you have to do is keep up the good work, surround yourself with like-minded individuals, and keep on expanding yourself though personal development.

Do not be afraid. You are never alone. The inner soul aspect of yourself will never die. So, while you are here engaged in play-based learning at Earth school, remember who you really are so you can have the most fun on this adventure of a lifetime. Pretend everyone on Earth is playing a game of freeze tag and the ones frozen are in a deep hypnotic slumber moving about like zombies without their soul's guidance. The only reason they are zombies is because they don't have a connection to the soul that is living right inside of them. You, the one who is awake, gets to tap as many zombies on the shoulder as possible to unfreeze them from the deep sleep of forgetfulness. As soon as you tap them with the glimmer of light, the trance melts into nothingness and the warmth of their own torch ignites into full blaze. With each awakened being, the game begins to take a turn for the lighter side. The ripple effect is grand and soon the blanket of light warms the whole globe uniting the beings of the planet. What was once a tyranny of fear blossoms into a freedom of love and life.

Mathematically, each human has the capacity to affect the world population in one lifetime through the exponential power of the ripple effect. A working mom will have access to X amount of people through her connections to employees, bosses, partners, and members of her social media. She has circles of influence through past classmates, workers, friends, family, service providers, volunteer ventures, and spiritual communities. Her positive impact on these people sends them back into their respective circles of influence to ripple out repeatedly until her light of consciousness spreads like wild-fire. There are so many groups of people waking up to the power of the inner presence and uniting across the world. Find out what topic turns you on and join a local or global group that empowers you to stay awake. Find us on Facebook with details at the end of the book.

Most importantly, the biggest service you are providing by doing the grand inner work is the guidance you are offering your awakened child. Self-development refines your leadership ability as a queen to hold the light for others to know the truth of their own light. Empower yourself, your family, child, and community to rise alongside you so everyone will be in good company. Depending on where your attention is placed, the world can appear to be a terrifying place to exist. There is an overwhelming amount of information to defend why someone should be fearful to be alive. And still, there is an avalanche of evidence to prove the infinite and omnipresent level of love and life-giving energy is available everywhere all at once. Can we afford another generation of humans whose divine identity is suppressed from their own consciousness? How much longer are we willing to let the net of fear hold down humanity? The slight shift in mental focus followed by a dedicated lifestyle in alignment with the truth can empower anyone to morph into the influential being that is their birthright. Let us all hold open the enlightened pathway for future generations to extend this great work further into the leading edge. It begins now.

Further Reading

The Four Agreements by Don Miguel Ruiz

The Seven Spiritual Laws of Success by Deepak Chopra

The Power of Now by Eckhart Tolle

The Crystal Children by Doreen Virtue

Heal Your Body by Louise Hay

The Alchemist by Paulo Coelho

Spiritual Liberation by Michael Bernard Beckwith

Acknowledgments

This book was made possible because of Angela Lauria, my incredible coach. Her ability to see straight into my soul and recognize my potential was incredible. Add on top of that her sense of humor and a no nonsense/shoot-from-the-hip way of delivering her messages, and it was a perfect blend for me. I remember sharing my vision of touring colleges talking to girls empowering them to live their soul purpose. It was a wonderful goal, yet it wasn't the right timing in my life. What she did next was life altering. She called me out of the closet and said, *"Mary, you're woowoo. So be woowoo. Do you really want to put on a suit every day and tour the country more days than you are home when you have two little children?"* She hit the nail on the head. No, I didn't realize the reality of what I was wishing for. She could have gotten me there, if that was for my highest good, but it wasn't at that point of my life. She gave me permission that I didn't know I needed. I thought I was way beyond needing to be liked or accepted. That's what an excellent coach is for: to shine the light on the places you can't yet see. She held the space, showed me the ropes, and voilà , we birthed a book to start a movement and change the world. For that, I am eternally grateful. The more I step up and out, the more I can serve others by holding the space for them to do the same.

To the Morgan James Publishing team: Special thanks to David Hancock, CEO & Founder for believing in me and my message. To my Author Relations Manager, Gayle West, thanks for making the process seamless and easy. Many more thanks to everyone else, but especially Jim Howard, Bethany Marshall, and Nickcole Watkins.

To my spiritual teacher, Reverend Michael Bernanrd Beckwith. Thank you for being a role model, leader and physical embodiment of the Truth. Each day, I fill my mind and practices with your teachings. It has allowed me to birth myself into a perpetual state of service and love. There's no other way I'd rather be.

To my soul posse, goddess sisters, and tribe of women who make up my village of support, thank you. Suzy Elsamanoudi, Amy Tan, Amy Kim, Corrin Moscowicz, Jessica Rader, Jessica Houghton, Agiya Vanaga, Lisa Garlough, Darcy Blank, Angelita Weber, Joleen Carmona, Rebecca Kellogge, Janice McDonald, Ressel Yu, Tina Landrum, and Harriett Knight. I appreciate all of your unconditional love, light, energy, and vision. You hold the space for my ability to birth light into this world with greater ease and grace. I love you!

To my parents and to my brother, Jimmy Huang. Thank you for being my first loves, protectors, and inspiration to grow past my boundaries. Without that, I would not be where I am today. Thank you to my extended family, Alex, Genny, Andrew, Gennina, and Andre Tan for being in my life.

To Adrian Tan, my beloved husband. I am so lucky to have you in my life. Your support, encouragement, and unconditional love are everything to me. Your devotion to self-development is an inspiration. Thank you for being an amazing partner, co-creator, and father. Life is sweeter because of you. Together we are unstoppable.

Lastly, to my gorgeous little light warriors, Arianna and Angelina Tan. You two are my teachers who inspire me to step into my greatness for the highest good. Thank you for showing me how to be my best self and how to shine. I do it all for you.

About the Author

Mary Tan is the founder of the Light Warrior School, an institution for children, and she is the creator of the Optimal Human Development with 8 Pillars of study. With more than a decade of coaching and speaking experience, she loves helping conscious moms coach their sensitive children through life challenges with greater ease and confidence. Mary's mission is to raise the next generation of soul-guided leaders. Teaching emotional intelligence, expanded awareness, and the spiritual laws of success are a few of the key practices. Mary graduated from New York University with a degree in Psychology and is a certified Neuro-Linguisitc Programming (NLP) life coach through the Christopher Howard

Training program. She studied the psychic arts through Illuminate Your Life, is certified in Reiki level II, and practices soul level healing through the Akashic records. Mary has integrated the wisdom of the ages with the truths of the universe to guide you and your child onto a path of greater meaning. Anything less than living your soul's purpose is a recipe for deep-seated unhappiness. She lives in Southern California with her husband raising two little light warriors of her own. When she's not empowering moms and children to live their best lives, she's scoping out the next international city to visit with her family. Otherwise, you'll find her having a salsa dance party in the living room with her two little girls.

Websites:

www.MaryTanEmpowers.com

www.LightWarriorSchool.com

Email:

Mary@MaryTanEmpowers.com

Facebook:

https://www.facebook.com/groups/TheEmpoweredChild/

Thank You

Congratulations Queen, you've completed the book! This is just the beginning of our amazing journey together. Let's stay connected and surround you with a tribe of empowered women awakened to the leader within. Keeping the conversation of conscious parenting alive with the support of your tribe will make it feel like you've got the backing of a village behind you. This is a movement to raise the next generation of emotionally intelligent leaders, and together we can take this to new heights.

JOIN OUR TRIBE:

go to https://www.facebook.com/groups/TheEmpoweredChild/

BONUS VIDEO SERIES: I have a three-part video series demonstrating how to teach your child a few of the tools mentioned in this book. Watch these fun videos with your child and learn how to live a more empowered life. Go to www.MaryTanEmpowers.com to claim them today.

If you've enjoyed this book be sure to share the light with other moms who can use some light in their lives, and write a review. I'd love to hear from you, too! You can post your comments on the Facebook group or email me at the address below.

I can always be reached through my website at

www.MaryTanEmpowers.com

or by email at

Mary@MaryTanEmpowers.com.

Here's to raising the next generation of empowered leaders!

With lots of love!

Mary Tan

Morgan James
Speakers Group

➤ www.TheMorganJamesSpeakersGroup.com

We connect Morgan James published authors with live and online events and audiences who will benefit from their expertise.

Morgan James makes all of our titles available
through the Library for All Charity Organization.

www.LibraryForAll.org

Printed in the USA
CPSIA information can be obtained
at www.ICGtesting.com
JSHW022344140824
68134JS00019B/1680